SECOND EDITION

TOP NOTCH

English for Today's World

3

Joan Saslow • Allen Ascher

With *Top Notch Pop Songs and Karaoke*
by Rob Morsberger

Top Notch: English for Today's World 3, Second Edition

Pearson Education, 10 Bank Street, White Plains, NY 10606

Staff credits: The people who made up the *Top Notch 3* team—representing editorial, design, production, and manufacturing—are Rhea Banker, Elizabeth Carlson, Aerin Csigay, Dave Dickey, Warren Fischbach, Aliza Greenblatt, Gosia Jaros-White, Ray Keating, Mike Kemper, and Wendy Wolf.

Cover design: Rhea Banker
Cover photo: Sprint/Corbis
Text design: Elizabeth Carlson
Text composition: Quarasan!

Library of Congress Cataloging-in-Publication Data

Saslow, Joan M.
  Top notch : English for today's world / Joan Saslow, Allen Ascher ; with Top Notch pop songs and Karaoke by
  Rob Morsberger. — 2nd ed.
     p. cm.
  ISBN 0-13-246988-X (set) — ISBN 0-13-247038-1 (v. 1) — ISBN 0-13-247048-9 (v. 2) — ISBN 0-13-247027-6
  (v. 3) 1. English language — Textbooks for foreign speakers. 2. English language — Problems, exercises, etc.
  I. Ascher, Allen. II. Title.
PE1128.S2757 2011
428.2'4 — dc22
                                                           2010019162

Photo credits: All original photography by Sharon Hoogstraten and David Mager. Page 2 Peter Widmann/Photolibrary.com; 5 (left) Laurence Mouton/PhotoAlto/Corbis, (bottom right) Shutterstock.com, 8 (mat) Shutterstock.com; 9 Will & Deni McIntyre/Getty Images; 10 Shutterstock.com; 13 (background) Shutterstock.com, (middle left) Shutterstock.com, (middle right) Shutterstock.com, (bottom left) Shutterstock.com; 15 (bottom right) Shutterstock.com; 17 (left) PhotoAlto/Alamy, (right) iStockphoto.com; 18 (left to right) Shutterstock.com, Shutterstock.com, Pearson Education/PH College, Maxine Hall/Corbis, Fotolia.com; 19 (right) Shutterstock.com; 20 (top left) Shutterstock.com, (top middle) Bubbles Photolibrary/Alamy, (top right) Phil Schermeister/Corbis, (bottom left) Shutterstock.com, (bottom right) Shutterstock.com, 22 (background) iStockphoto.com, (ragweed) Shutterstock.com, (bacteria) Shutterstock.com; 23 (background) Shutterstock.com; 25 (top) Inspirestock/Corbis, (middle) Shutterstock.com, (bottom) iStockphoto.com; 26 Shutterstock.com; 27 (top middle) Shutterstock.com; 31 (bottom) Shutterstock.com; 32 (bottom right) Shutterstock.com; 33 Corbis Premium RF/Alamy; 34 (card) Shutterstock.com, (caterer) Stewart Cohen/Getty Images, (bottom right) Serge Kozak/Corbis; 37 (background) Shutterstock.com, (bottom left) Shutterstock.com; 40 Shutterstock.com; 43 Shutterstock.com; 44 (curl) Shutterstock.com, (aloud) Shutterstock.com, (listen) Shutterstock.com, (do) Shutterstock.com, (online) Shutterstock.com, (e-books) AP Images/Joerg Sarbach; 45 Shutterstock.com; 46 (top) Marvel; 47 (bottom) Shutterstock.com; 49 (background) Shutterstock.com; 50 (top left) The Granger Collection, (top right) Mandel Ngan/AFP/Getty Images, (bottom left) Bettmann/Corbis, (tv) Shutterstock.com; 51 (flood) Shutterstock.com; 53 (background) Shutterstock.com, (top) Shutterstock.com, (bottom) Shutterstock.com; 54 South Florida Sun-Sentinel. Reprinted with permission; 56 China Photos/Getty Images; 58 (background) Shutterstock.com, (left) Dorling Kindersley, (right) Dorling Kindersley, 59 (all) Dorling Kindersley; 62 (top to bottom) C Squared Studios/Getty Images, Siede Preis/Getty Images, Olympus America Inc., Siede Preis/Getty Images, Shutterstock.com; 63 (bottom) Shutterstock.com; 68 Benelux Press/Index Stock Imagery; 70 John Lund/Sam Diephuis/Photolibrary.com; 74 (top left) Photo Japan/Alamy, (bottom left) Hong Suk-young and Son Kwan-soo, (top right) Tony Freeman/PhotoEdit Inc., (middle right) Jeremy Woodhouse/Photolibrary.com, (bottom right) Shutterstock.com; 76 (cake) Michael Newman/PhotoEdit Inc., (fireworks) Shutterstock.com, (parades) Chip East/Corbis, (picnics) Shutterstock.com, (pray) Zafer Kizilkaya/Coral Planet, (gifts) Shutterstock.com, (dead) Doug Martin/Photo Researchers, Inc., Philip Gould/Corbis, (costumes) 77 Shutterstock.com; 79 (top) James Hardy/Photolibrary.com, (bottom) Shutterstock.com; 80 (left) Mark Downey/Lucid Images, (top right) Steve Vidler/SuperStock, (bottom right) Pablo Corral/Corbis; 82 (left) Elyse Lewin/Getty Images, (middle) Stockbyte/SuperStock, (right) Darama/Corbis; 85 (background top) Shutterstock.com, (background bottom) Shutterstock.com, (middle left) Kevin Foy/Alamy, (middle right) Richard Powers/Corbis, (bottom right) AP Images/Ric Vasquez-Rumbo, (bottom middle) Bryan Smith/ZUMA Press/Newscom 86; (top left) Carl & Ann Purcell/Corbis, (top middle) Hulton Archive/Getty Images, (top right) Peter Arnold, Inc./Alamy, (middle) Keith Morris/Alamy, (bottom left) Shutterstock.com, (bottom right) iStockphoto.com; 87 (backgrounds) Shutterstock.com; 94 (top left) North Wind Picture Archives, (top right) Science & Society Picture Library, (bottom) Martin Paul Ltd./Index Stock Imagery; 95 (left to right) Alinari/Art Resource, NY, Chris Livingston/Getty Images, Ray Ellis/Photo Researchers, Inc., H. Armstrong Roberts/ClassicStock/Corbis, Shutterstock.com; 97 (background top) Shutterstock.com, (background bottom) Shutterstock.com, (wagon) Carl & Ann Purcell/Corbis, (potter's) Blair Seitz/Photo Researchers, Inc., (carts) Bettmann/Corbis, (chariot) The Art Archive/Bibliotheque des Arts Decoratifs Paris/Dagli Orti, (auto) Ron Kimball/Ron Kimball Stock. All rights reserved, (middle) Shutterstock.com; 98 Shutterstock.com; 99 (bottom) Inmagine/Alamy; 103 Shutterstock.com; 104 NASA/Corbis; 107 Shutterstock.com; 109 (bottom) Image100/Alamy; 110 (background) Shutterstock.com, (top) James Hardy/Photolibrary.com; 111 (backgrounds) Shutterstock.com; 113 (left top) Dave Jacobs/Photolibrary.com, (left bottom) Shutterstock.com, (bottom middle) Corbis Premium RF/Alamy, (bottom right) Lonely Planet/SuperStock; 114 (snake) Shutterstock.com, (shark) Shutterstock.com, (jellyfish) Shutterstock.com, (bear) Shutterstock.com, (scorpion) Shutterstock.com, (mosquito) Shutterstock.com; 116 (forest) Jim Steinberg/Photo Researchers, Inc., (jungle) Gregory G. Dimijian/Photo Researchers, Inc., (valley) John Lamb/Getty Images, (canyon) T. Gervis/Robert Harding Picture Library, (island) Don Hebert/Getty Images, (glacier) Shutterstock.com, (mountainous) Fotolia.com, (hilly) David Weintraub/Photo Researchers, Inc., (flat) Jim Steinberg/Photo Researchers, Inc., (dry) Shutterstock.com, (lush) WONG SZE FEI/Fotolia; 117 (top left) Alison Wright/Corbis, (bottom left) True North Images/agefotostock, (middle) Shutterstock.com, (top right) N. DeVore III/Bruce Coleman, Inc., (bottom right) Yoshio Tomii Photo Studio/Photolibrary.com; p. 118 (left) Shutterstock.com, (right) Shutterstock.com; 121 (top left) Shutterstock.com, (middle left) Don Pitcher/Photolibrary.com, (bottom right) Uppercut Images/Photolibrary.com.

Illustration credits: Steve Attoe, pp. 30, 92, 114, 115; Sue Carlson, pp. 110, 112, 113, 120, 121; Mark Collins, p. 92; Brian Hughes, p. 54; Robert McPhillips, p. 49; Andy Myer, pp. 65, 102; Tom Newsom, pp. 25, 61, 73, 109; Dusan Petricic, pp. 16, 24, 120; Gail Piazza, p. 14; Anne Veltfort, p. 35.

Text credits: Page 10 Article on dinner party etiquette; Antique Digest—"Old and Sold Antique Auction," www.oldandsold.com <http://www.oldandsold.com/>; Page 26 color survey, Information Please®, 2009 Pearson, Inc. All rights reserved.

Printed in the United States of America

ISBN-10: 0-13-246987-1
ISBN-13: 978-0-13-246987-6
10 11 – V082 – 17 16 15 14

ISBN-10: 0-13-247027-6 (with MyEnglishLab)
ISBN-13: 978-0-13-247027-8 (with MyEnglishLab)
5 6 7 8 9 10 – V082 – 17 16 15 14 13

About the Authors

Joan Saslow

Joan Saslow has taught in a variety of programs in South America and the United States. She is author of a number of multi-level integrated-skills courses for adults and young adults: *Ready to Go: Language, Lifeskills, and Civics; Workplace Plus: Living and Working in English;* and of *Literacy Plus*. She is also author of *English in Context: Reading Comprehension for Science and Technology*. Ms. Saslow was the series director of *True Colors* and *True Voices*. She participates in the English Language Specialist Program in the U.S. Department of State's Bureau of Educational and Cultural Affairs.

Allen Ascher

Allen Ascher has been a teacher and a teacher trainer in China and the United States and taught in the TESOL Certificate Program at the New School in New York. He was also academic director of the International English Language Institute at Hunter College. Mr. Ascher is author of the "Teaching Speaking" module of *Teacher Development Interactive*, an online multimedia teacher-training program, and of *Think about Editing: A Grammar Editing Guide for ESL*.

Both Ms. Saslow and Mr. Ascher are frequent and popular speakers at professional conferences and international gatherings of EFL and ESL teachers.

Authors' Acknowledgments

The authors are indebted to these reviewers who provided extensive and detailed feedback and suggestions for the second edition of *Top Notch* as well as the hundreds of teachers who participated in surveys and focus groups.

Manuel Aguilar Díaz, El Cultural Trujillo, Peru • **Manal Al Jordi,** Expression Training Company, Kuwait • **José Luis Ames Portocarrero,** El Cultural Arequipa, Peru • **Vanessa de Andrade,** CCBEU Inter Americano, Curitiba, Brazil • **Rossana Aragón Castro,** ICPNA Cusco, Peru • **Jennifer Ballesteros,** Universidad del Valle de México, Campus Tlalpan, Mexico City, Mexico • **Brad Bawtinheimer,** PROULEX, Guadalajara, Mexico • **Carolina Bermeo,** Universidad Central, Bogotá, Colombia • **Zulma Buitrago,** Universidad Pedagógica Nacional, Bogotá, Colombia • **Fabiola R. Cabello,** Idiomas Católica, Lima, Peru • **Emma Campo Collante,** Universidad Central Bogotá, Colombia • **Viviane de Cássia Santos Carlini,** Spectrum Line, Pouso Alegre, Brazil • **Fanny Castelo,** ICPNA Cusco, Peru • **José Luis Castro Moreno,** Universidad de León, Mexico • **Mei Chia-Hong,** Southern Taiwan University (STUT), Taiwan • **Guven Ciftci,** Faith University, Turkey • **Freddy Correa Montenegro,** Centro Colombo Americano, Cali, Colombia • **Alicia Craman de Carmand,** Idiomas Católica, Lima, Peru • **Jesús G. Díaz Osío,** Florida National College, Miami, USA • **Ruth Domínguez,** Universidad Central Bogotá, Colombia • **Roxana Echave,** El Cultural Arequipa, Peru • **Angélica Escobar Chávez,** Universidad de León, Mexico • **John Fieldeldy,** College of Engineering, Nihon University, Aizuwakamatsu-shi, Japan • **Herlinda Flores,** Centro de Idiomas Universidad Veracruzana, Mexico • **Claudia Franco,** Universidad Pedagógica Nacional, Colombia • **Andrea Fredricks,** Embassy CES, San Francisco, USA • **Chen-Chen Fu,** National Kaoshiung First Science Technology University, Taiwan • **María Irma Gallegos Peláez,** Universidad del Valle de México, Mexico City, Mexico • **Carolina García Carbajal,** El Cultural Arequipa, Peru • **Claudia Gavancho Terrazas,** ICPNA Cusco, Peru • **Adriana Gómez,** Centro Colombo Americano, Bogotá, Colombia • **Raphaël Goossens,** ICPNA Cusco, Peru • **Carlo Granados,** Universidad Central, Bogotá, Colombia • **Ralph Grayson,** Idiomas Católica, Lima, Peru • **Murat Gultekin,** Fatih University, Turkey • **Monika Hennessey,** ICPNA Chiclayo, Peru • **Lidia Hernández Medina,** Universidad del Valle de México, Mexico City, Mexico • **Jesse Huang,** National Central University, Taiwan • **Eric Charles Jones,** Seoul University of Technology, South Korea • **Jun-Chen Kuo,** Tajen University, Taiwan • **Susan Krieger,** Embassy CES, San Francisco, USA • **Robert Labelle,** Centre for Training and Development, Dawson College, Canada • **Erin Lemaistre,** Chung-Ang University, South Korea • **Eleanor S. Leu,** Soochow University, Taiwan • **Yihui Li (Stella Li),** Fooyin University, Taiwan • **Chin-Fan Lin,** Shih Hsin University, Taiwan • **Linda Lin,** Tatung Institute of Technology, Taiwan • **Kristen Lindblom,** Embassy CES, San Francisco, USA • **Ricardo López,** PROULEX, Guadalajara, Mexico • **Neil Macleod,** Kansai Gaidai University, Osaka, Japan • **Robyn McMurray,** Pusan National University, South Korea • **Paula Medina,** London Language Institute, Canada • **María Teresa Meléndez de Elorreaga,** ICPNA Chiclayo, Peru • **Sandra Cecilia Mora Espejo,** Universidad del Valle de México, Campus Tlalpan, Mexico City, Mexico • **Ricardo Nausa,** Centro Colombo Americano, Bogotá, Colombia • **Tim Newfields,** Tokyo University Faculty of Economics, Tokyo, Japan • **Mónica Nomberto,** ICPNA Chiclayo, Peru • **Scarlett Ostojic,** Idiomas Católica, Lima, Peru • **Ana Cristina Ochoa,** CCBEU Inter Americano, Curitiba, Brazil • **Doralba Pérez,** Universidad Pedagógica Nacional, Bogotá, Colombia • **David Perez Montalvo,** ICPNA Cusco, Peru • **Wahrena Elizabeth Pfeister,** University of Suwon, South Korea • **Wayne Allen Pfeister,** University of Suwon, South Korea • **Cecilia Ponce de León,** ICPNA Cusco, Peru • **Andrea Rebonato,** CCBEU Inter Americano, Curitiba, Brazil • **Elizabeth Rodríguez López,** El Cultural Trujillo, Peru • **Olga Rodríguez Romero,** El Cultural Trujillo, Peru • **Timothy Samuelson,** BridgeEnglish, Denver, USA • **Enrique Sánchez Guzmán,** PROULEX, Guadalajara, Mexico • **Letícia Santos,** ICBEU Ibiá, Brazil • **Lyndsay Shaeffer,** Embassy CES, San Francisco, USA • **John Eric Sherman,** Hong Ik University, South Korea • **João Vitor Soares,** NACC, São Paulo, Brazil • **Elena Sudakova,** English Language Center, Kiev, Ukraine • **Richard Swingle,** Kansai Gaidai College, Osaka, Japan • **Sandrine Ting,** St. John's University, Taiwan • **Shu-Ping Tsai,** Fooyin University, Taiwan • **José Luis Urbina Hurtado,** Universidad de León, Mexico • **Monica Urteaga,** Idiomas Católica, Lima, Peru • **Juan Carlos Villafuerte,** ICPNA Cusco, Peru • **Dr. Wen-hsien Yang,** National Kaohsiung Hospitality College, Kaohsiung, Taiwan • **Holger Zamora,** ICPNA Cusco, Peru.

Learning Objectives

Unit	Communication Goals	Vocabulary	Grammar
1 **Make Small Talk** page 2	• Make small talk • Describe a busy schedule • Develop your cultural awareness • Discuss how culture changes over time	• Ways to ask about proper address • Intensifiers • Manners and etiquette	• Tag questions: usage, form, and common errors • The past perfect: meaning, form, and usage **GRAMMAR BOOSTER** • Tag questions: short answers • Verb usage: present and past (review)
2 **Health Matters** page 14	• Call in sick • Make a medical or dental appointment • Discuss types of treatments • Talk about medications	• Dental emergencies • Symptoms • Medical procedures • Types of medical treatments • Medications	• Modal <u>must</u>: drawing conclusions • <u>Will be able to</u> • Modals <u>may</u> and <u>might</u> **GRAMMAR BOOSTER** • Other ways to draw conclusions: <u>probably</u>; <u>most likely</u>; common errors • Expressing possibility with <u>maybe</u>; common errors
3 **Getting Things Done** page 26	• Get someone else to do something • Request express service • Evaluate the quality of service • Plan a meeting or social event	• Ways to help out another person • Ways to indicate acceptance • Services • Planning an event	• Causatives <u>get</u>, <u>have</u>, and <u>make</u> • The passive causative **GRAMMAR BOOSTER** • <u>Let</u> to indicate permission • Causative <u>have</u>: common errors • The passive causative: the <u>by</u> phrase
4 **Reading for Pleasure** page 38	• Recommend a book • Offer to lend something • Describe your reading habits • Discuss the quality of reading materials	• Types of books • Ways to describe a book • Ways to enjoy reading	• Noun clauses: usage, form, and common errors • Noun clauses: embedded questions ◦ Form and common errors **GRAMMAR BOOSTER** • Verbs and adjectives that can be followed by clauses with <u>that</u> • Embedded questions: usage and common errors, punctuation, with infinitives • Noun clauses as subjects and objects

5 **Natural Disasters** page 50	• Convey a message
	• Report news
	• Describe natural disasters
	• Prepare for an emergency
		• Severe weather and other natural disasters
		• Adjectives of severity
		• Emergency preparations and supplies
			• Indirect speech:
			  ◦ Imperatives
			  ◦ <u>Say</u> and <u>tell</u>
			  ◦ Tense changes
			
			GRAMMAR BOOSTER
			• Direct speech: punctuation rules
			• Indirect speech: optional tense changes
			  ◦ Form and common errors

Conversation Strategies	Listening / Pronunciation	Reading	Writing
• Talk about the weather to begin a conversation with someone you don't know • Use question tags to encourage someone to make small talk • Ask about how someone wants to be addressed • Answer a <u>Do you mind</u> question with <u>Absolutely not</u> to indicate agreement • Say <u>That was nothing</u> to indicate that something even more surprising happened • Use <u>Wow!</u> to indicate that you are impressed	**Listening Skills:** • Listen for main ideas • Listen to summarize • Confirm the correct paraphrases **Pronunciation:** • Rising and falling intonation of tag questions	**Texts:** • A business meeting memo and agenda • A magazine article about formal dinner etiquette of the past • A survey about culture change • A photo story **Skills/Strategies:** • Predict • Confirm facts • Summarize	**Task:** • Write a formal and an informal e-mail message **WRITING BOOSTER** • Formal e-mail etiquette
• Introduce disappointing information with <u>I'm afraid …</u> • Express disappointment with <u>I'm sorry to hear that</u> • Show concern with <u>Is something wrong?</u> and <u>That must be awful</u> • Begin a request for assistance with <u>I wonder if …</u> • Use <u>Let's see …</u> to indicate you are checking for something • Confirm an appointment with <u>I'll / We'll see you then</u> • Express emphatic thanks with <u>I really appreciate it</u>	**Listening Skills:** • Auditory discrimination • Listen for details **Pronunciation:** • Intonation of lists	**Texts:** • A travel tips website about dental emergencies • A brochure about choices in medical treatments • A patient information form • A medicine label • A photo story **Skills/Strategies:** • Understand from context • Relate to personal experience • Draw conclusions	**Task:** • Write an essay comparing two types of medical treatments **WRITING BOOSTER** • Comparisons and contrasts
• Use <u>I would, but …</u> and an excuse to politely turn down a request • Indicate acceptance of someone's excuse with <u>That's OK. I understand</u> • Suggest an alternative with <u>Maybe you could …</u> • Soften a request by beginning it with <u>Do you think you could …</u> • Soften an almost certain <u>no</u> with <u>That might be difficult</u> • Use <u>Well, …</u> to indicate willingness to reconsider	**Listening Skills:** • Listen for specific information • Listen for main ideas • Listen for order of details • Listen to summarize **Pronunciation:** • Emphatic stress to express enthusiasm	**Texts:** • A survey about procrastination • A travel article about tailoring services • A photo story **Skills/Strategies:** • Identify supporting details • Activate language from a text	**Task:** • Write an essay expressing a point of view about procrastination **WRITING BOOSTER** • Supporting an opinion with personal examples
• Use <u>Actually</u> to show appreciation for someone's interest in a topic • Soften a question with <u>Could you tell me …?</u> • Indicate disappointment with <u>Too bad</u> • Use <u>I'm dying to …</u> to indicate extreme interest • Say <u>That would be great</u> to express gratitude for someone's willingness to do something	**Listening Skills:** • Listen to take notes • Listen to infer a speaker's point of view and support your opinion **Pronunciation:** • Sentence stress in short answers with <u>so</u>	**Texts:** • An online bookstore website • Capsule descriptions of four best-sellers • A magazine article about comics • A photo story **Skills/Strategies:** • Recognize points of view • Critical thinking	**Task:** • Write a summary and review of something you've read **WRITING BOOSTER** • Summarizing
• Use <u>I would, but …</u> to politely turn down an offer • Say <u>Will do</u> to agree to a request for action • Use <u>Well</u> to begin providing requested information • Say <u>What a shame</u> to show empathy for a misfortune • Introduce reassuring contrasting information with <u>But, …</u> • Say <u>Thank goodness for that</u> to indicate relief	**Listening Skills:** • Listen for main ideas • Listen for details • Listen to paraphrase • Listen to infer meaning **Pronunciation:** • Direct and indirect speech: rhythm	**Texts:** • News headlines • A textbook article about earthquakes • Statistical charts • A photo story **Skills/Strategies:** • Paraphrase • Confirm facts • Identify cause and effect • Interpret data from a chart	**Task:** • Write a procedure for how to prepare for an emergency **WRITING BOOSTER** • Organizing detail statements by order of importance

Conversation Strategies	Listening / Pronunciation	Reading	Writing
• Say <u>No kidding!</u> to indicate delight or surprise • Say <u>How come?</u> to ask for a reason • Express a regret with <u>I should have …</u> • Use <u>You never know...</u> to reassure someone • Accept another's reassurance with <u>True</u>	**Listening Skills:** • Listen to infer a speaker's motives • Listen for details • Listen to classify information **Pronunciation:** • Reduction of <u>have</u> in perfect modals	**Texts:** • Career and skills inventories • A magazine article with tips for effective work habits • A photo story **Skills/Strategies:** • Understand from context • Confirm content	**Task:** • Write a short autobiography **WRITING BOOSTER** • Dividing an essay into topics
• Show friendliness by wishing someone a good holiday • Reciprocate good wishes with <u>Thanks! Same to you!</u> • Preface a potentially sensitive question with <u>Do you mind if I ask you …</u> • Ask about socially appropriate behavior in order to avoid embarrassment • Express appreciation with <u>Thanks. That's really helpful</u>	**Listening Skills:** • Listen for the main idea • Listen for details • Infer information **Pronunciation:** • "Thought groups"	**Texts:** • A magazine article about holidays around the world • Proverbs about weddings • Factoids on holidays • A photo story **Skills/Strategies:** • Preview • Scan for facts • Compare and contrast • Relate to personal experience	**Task:** • Write a detailed description of two holidays **WRITING BOOSTER** • Descriptive details
• Congratulate someone for a major new purchase • Apologize for lateness and provide an explanation • Indicate regret for a mistake by beginning an explanation with <u>I'm ashamed to say …</u> • Reduce another's self-blame with <u>That can happen to anyone</u> and <u>No harm done</u>	**Listening Skills:** • Infer the correct adjective • Listen for main ideas • Listen to associate • Listen to infer meaning **Pronunciation:** • Contractions with <u>'d</u> in spoken English	**Texts:** • Case studies of poor purchasing decisions • A book excerpt about the printing press • Factoids on famous inventions • A photo story **Skills/Strategies:** • Infer information • Identify cause and effect	**Task:** • Write an essay about the historical impact of an important invention **WRITING BOOSTER** • Summary statements
• Ask for permission when bringing up a sticky subject • Politely indicate unwillingness with <u>No offense, but …</u> • Apologize for refusing with <u>I hope you don't mind</u> • Use <u>How do you feel about...</u> to invite someone's opinion • Use <u>Well, …</u> to introduce a different point of view • Use <u>So …</u> to begin a question clarifying someone's statement	**Listening Skills:** • Infer a speaker's political and social beliefs • Infer a speaker's point of view • Listen to summarize • Auditory discrimination **Pronunciation:** • Stress to emphasize meaning	**Texts:** • A self-test of political literacy • A textbook introduction to global problems • A photo story **Skills/Strategies:** • Activate language from a text • Understand from context • Critical thinking	**Task:** • Write an essay presenting the two sides of a controversial issue **WRITING BOOSTER** • Contrasting ideas
• Show interest in someone's plans by asking follow-up questions • Indicate possible intention with <u>I've been thinking about it</u> • Qualify a positive response with <u>Sure, but …</u> • Elaborate further information using <u>Well, …</u> • Express gratitude for a warning	**Listening Skills:** • Infer a speaker's point of view • Listen for main ideas • Listen for details • Listen to summarize **Pronunciation:** • Voiced and voiceless <u>th</u>	**Texts:** • Maps • A magazine article about ways to curb global warming • A photo story **Skills/Strategies:** • Interpret maps • Understand from context • Critical thinking • Summarize	**Task:** • Write a geographic description of your country, state, or province **WRITING BOOSTER** • Organizing by spatial relations

To the Teacher

What is *Top Notch*?

Top Notch is a six-level* communicative course that prepares adults and young adults to interact successfully and confidently with both native and non-native speakers of English.

The goal of the *Top Notch* course is to make English unforgettable through:

► Multiple exposures to new language
► Numerous opportunities to practice it
► Deliberate and intensive recycling

The *Top Notch* course has two beginning levels: *Top Notch* Fundamentals for true beginners and *Top Notch* 1 for false beginners.

Each full level of *Top Notch* contains enough material for 60 to 90 hours of classroom instruction. A wide choice of supplementary components makes it easy to tailor *Top Notch* to the needs of your classes.

Summit 1 and *Summit 2* are the titles of the fifth and sixth levels of the *Top Notch* course. All Student's Books are available in split editions with bound-in workbooks.

The *Top Notch* instructional design

Daily confirmation of progress

Each easy-to-follow two-page lesson begins with a clearly stated communication goal. All lesson activities are integrated with the goal and systematically build toward a final speaking activity in which students demonstrate achievement of the goal. "Can-do" statements in each unit ensure students' awareness of the continuum of their progress.

A purposeful conversation syllabus

Memorable conversation models provide essential and practical social language that students can carry "in their pockets" for use in real life. Guided conversation pair work enables students to modify, personalize, and extend each model so they can use it to communicate their <u>own</u> thoughts and needs. Free discussion activities are carefully crafted so students can continually retrieve and use the language from the models. All conversation models are informed by the Longman Corpus of Spoken American English.

An emphasis on cultural fluency

Recognizing that English is a global language, *Top Notch* actively equips students to interact socially with people from a variety of cultures and deliberately prepares them to understand accented speakers from diverse language backgrounds.

Intensive vocabulary development

Students actively work with a rich vocabulary of high-frequency words, collocations, and expressions in all units of the Student's Book. Clear illustrations and definitions clarify meaning and provide support for independent study, review, and test preparation. Systematic recycling promotes smooth and continued acquisition of vocabulary from the beginning to the advanced levels of the course.

A dynamic approach to grammar

An explicit grammar syllabus is supported by charts containing clear grammar rules, relevant examples, and explanations of meaning and use. Numerous grammar exercises provide focused practice, and grammar usage is continually activated in communication exercises that illustrate the grammar being learned.

A dedicated pronunciation syllabus

Focused pronunciation, rhythm, and intonation practice is included in each unit, providing application of each pronunciation point to the target language of the unit and facilitating comprehensible pronunciation.

ActiveBook

SECOND EDITION
TOP NOTCH
with ActiveBook
3

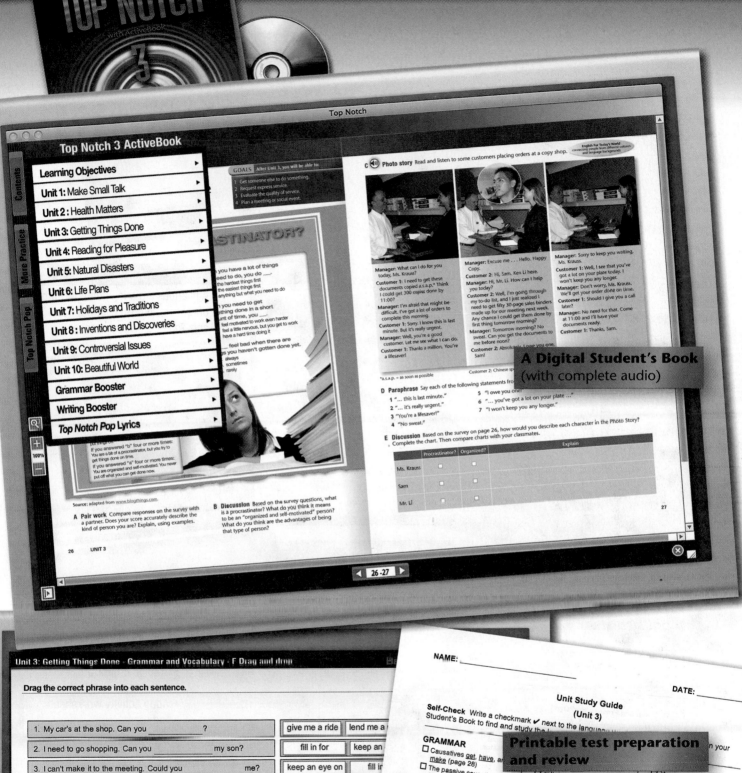

A Digital Student's Book
(with complete audio)

Interactive practice (with daily activity records)
- ► Extra listening and reading comprehension
- ► Record-yourself speaking
- ► Grammar and vocabulary practice
- ► Games and puzzles
- ► *Top Notch Pop* and karaoke

Printable test preparation and review

The Teacher's Edition and Lesson Planner

Includes:
- ▶ A bound-in Methods Handbook for professional development
- ▶ Detailed lesson plans with suggested teaching times
- ▶ Language, culture, and corpus notes
- ▶ Student's Book and Workbook answer keys
- ▶ Audioscripts
- ▶ *Top Notch TV* teaching notes

▶ ActiveTeach

- ▶ A Digital Student's Book with interactive whiteboard (IWB) software
- ▶ Instantly accessible audio and *Top Notch TV* video
- ▶ Interactive exercises from the Student's *ActiveBook* for in-class use
- ▶ A complete menu of printable extension activities

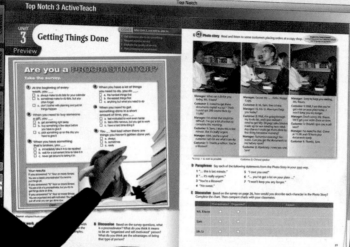

Top Notch TV

A hilarious situation comedy, authentic unrehearsed on-the-street interviews, and *Top Notch Pop* karaoke.

The Digital Student's Book
With zoom, write, highlight, save and other IWB tools.

Printable Extension Activities

Including:
- Writing process worksheets
- Vocabulary flashcards
- Learning strategies
- Graphic organizers
- Pronunciation activities
- Video activity worksheets and more . . .

Page 1 of 2

NAME: _____   DATE: _____

Writing Process Worksheet
(Accompanies Unit 3, page 36)

ASSIGNMENT: Write an explanation, giving examples from personal experience, of whether or not you are a procrastinator.

1. PREWRITING

Check the box that is true for you.

☐ I get things repaired as soon as they get damaged.	☐ I usually wait a few months to get something repaired.	☐ After a year or so, I ju... buy a new item.
☐ I get things cleaned right away.	☐ I wait until I need to wear something, then get it cleaned.	☐ Stuff just sits in my closet! I never get it cleaned.
☐ I always pay my bills on time.	☐ Every now and then, I'm a little late paying my bills.	☐ I can never seem to pay my bills on time.
☐ I plan my vacation months in advance.	☐ I like to plan vacations at the last minute, right before I leave.	☐ I never plan vacatio... I just get up and go!
☐ I'm really good about keeping in touch with people	☐ Sometimes I let a lot of time go by, but then send an e-mail or call my friends.	☐ I just can't seem to keep up with my frien...

NAME: _____

Learning Strategy
(Unit 10, page 118, Reading)

READING STRATEGY: identifying causes and effects

Understand the relationship between causes (why something happens or is true) and effects (results of the causes) to improve comprehension of a text.

PRACTICE

Fill in the chart with causes and effects from the Reading on page 118 in the Student's Book.

Causes	Effects
An increase in the amount of CO_2 in the air....	contributes to global warming.
Choosing clean energy....	
Replacing an old refrigerator or air-conditioner with an energy efficient model...	will use less gasoline and save money.
	will use 25% less electricity.
Using products that are recycled from old paper, glass, and metal...	
Shipping foods over long distances...	causes flooding in coastal areas...

Workbook

Workbook
Daily assignments that reinforce each lesson.

Classroom Audio Program

Classroom Audio Program
Includes a variety of authentic regional and non-native accents.

Complete Assessment Package

Complete Assessment Package
Ready-made achievement tests. Software provides option to edit, delete, or add items.

Full-Course Placement Tests

Full-Course Placement Tests
Choose printable or online version.

Copy & Go
Board games, role plays, information gaps, and "find someone who. . ." for every lesson.

MyTopNotchLab

An optional online learning tool with:

▶ An interactive *Top Notch* Workbook
▶ Speaking and writing activities
▶ Pop-up grammar help
▶ Student's Book *Grammar Booster* exercises
▶ *Top Notch TV* with extensive viewing activities
▶ Automatically-graded achievement tests
▶ Easy course management and record-keeping

Make small talk

GOALS After Unit 1, you will be able to:

1 Make small talk.
2 Describe a busy schedule.
3 Develop your cultural awareness.
4 Discuss how culture changes over time.

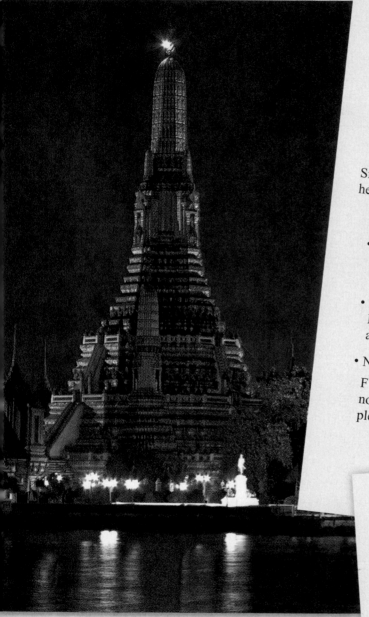

ROWAN PAPER
International

Annual Meeting for Affiliates
Bangkok, Thailand
March 24 – 27

Meeting Etiquette

WELCOME TO OUR AFFILIATES FROM
ALL PARTS OF THE WORLD!

Since we all come together from different traditions and cultures,
here are some guidelines to make this meeting run smoothly:

• Please arrive promptly for meetings.

• Dress is business casual: no ties or jackets required.
However, no denim or shorts, please. Ladies should feel free
to wear slacks.

• Please refrain from making or taking calls during meetings.
Put all cell phones and pagers on vibrate mode. If you have
an urgent call, please step outside into the corridor.

• Note: Everyone is on a first-name basis.

FYI: Food is international style. All meals will provide
non-meat options. If you have a special dietary requirement,
please speak with Ms. Parnthep at the front desk.

ROWAN PAPER
International

Agenda–March 24

8:30:	Breakfast buffet in Salon Bangkok	Ballroom
9:15:	Welcome and opening remarks Philippe Martin President and CEO	Ballroom
9:45:	First quarter results and discussion Angela de Groot CFO	
10:30:	Coffee break	Ballroom
11:00:	International outlook and integrated marketing plans Sergio Montenegro	
11:00:	Regional marketing plans • U.S. and Canada Group • Mexico and Central America Group • Caribbean Group • South America (Southern Cone and Andes) Group • Brazil	Salon A Salon B Salon C Salon D Salon E

A Read and summarize the etiquette guidelines
for an international business meeting. Write
four statements beginning with <u>Don't</u>.

B **Discussion** Why do you think Rowan Paper
International feels it's necessary to tell
participants about meeting etiquette? What
could happen if they didn't clarify expectations?

C 🔊))) **Photo story** Read and listen to a conversation between two participants at the meeting in Bangkok.

ENGLISH FOR TODAY'S WORLD
connecting people from different cultures
and language backgrounds

Teresa: Allow me to introduce myself. I am Teresa Segovia from the Santiago office. *Sawatdee-Kaa.*

Surat: Where did you learn the *wai**? You're Chilean, aren't you?

Teresa: Yes, I am. But I have a friend in Chile from Thailand.

Surat: Well, *Sawatdee-Khrab.* Nice to meet you, Ms. Segovia. I'm Surat Leekpai.

Teresa: No need to be so formal. Please call me Terri.

Surat: And please call me Surat.

Teresa: OK. Surat, do you mind my asking you a question about that, though?

Surat: Not at all.

Teresa: Is it customary in Thailand for people to be on a first-name basis?

Surat: Well, at company meetings in English, always. In other situations, though, people tend to be a little more formal. It's probably best to watch what others do. You know what they say: "When in Rome, . . . "

Teresa: Mm-hmm . . ., "do as the Romans do!"

Teresa: Spanish speaker / Surat: Thai speaker
*Thais greet each other with a gesture called the <u>wai</u> and by saying "Sawatdee-Kaa" (women) / "Sawatdee-Khrab" (men).

D Think and explain Answer the following questions.

1 Why was Surat surprised about the way Teresa greeted him? How do you know he was surprised?

2 Why do you think Teresa decided to say "Sawatdee-Kaa"?

3 What did Teresa mean when she said, "No need to be so formal"?

4 What do you think the difference is between "People *tend to be* a little more formal" and "People *are* a little more formal"?

5 What do you think the saying "When in Rome, do as the Romans do" means?

E Personalization Look at the chart. If you took a trip to another country, how would you like to be addressed? Explain your reasons.

I'd like to be called . . .	Always	In some situations	Never
by my title and my family name.	☐	☐	☐
by my first name.	☐	☐	☐
by my nickname.	☐	☐	☐
I'd prefer to follow the local customs.	☐	☐	☐
Other	☐	☐	☐

F Discussion Talk about the following questions.

1 In your opinion, is it inappropriate for two people of very different status (such as a CEO and an assistant) to be on a first-name basis? Explain.

2 In general, when do you think people should use first names with each other? When should they use titles and last names? Explain your reasons.

GOAL Make small talk

CONVERSATION MODEL

A 🔊 1:03 Read and listen to two people meeting and making small talk.

A: Good morning. Beautiful day, isn't it?

B: It really is. By the way, I'm Kazuko Toshinaga.

A: I'm Jane Quitt. Nice to meet you.

B: Nice to meet you, too.

A: Do you mind if I call you Kazuko?

B: Absolutely not. Please do.

A: And please call me Jane.

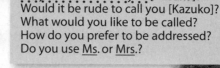

🔊 1:05 **Ways to ask about proper address**

Do you mind if I call you [Kazuko]?
Would it be rude to call you [Kazuko]?
What would you like to be called?
How do you prefer to be addressed?
Do you use <u>Ms.</u> or <u>Mrs.</u>?

B 🔊 1:04 **Rhythm and intonation** Listen again and repeat.
Then practice the Conversation Model with a partner.

GRAMMAR   Tag questions: use and form

Use tag questions to confirm information you already think is true or
to encourage someone to make small talk with you.
   (It's a) beautiful day, **isn't it?**

When the statement is affirmative, the tag is negative. When the
statement is negative, the tag is affirmative.

affirmative		negative	
You're Lee,	**aren't you?**	You're not Amy,	**are you?**
She speaks Thai,	**doesn't she?**	I don't know you,	**do I?**
He's going to drive,	**isn't he?**	We're not going to eat here,	**are we?**
They'll be here later,	**won't they?**	It won't be long,	**will it?**
You were there,	**weren't you?**	He wasn't driving,	**was he?**
They left,	**didn't they?**	We didn't know,	**did we?**
It's been a great day,	**hasn't it?**	She hasn't been here long,	**has she?**
Ann would like Quito,	**wouldn't she?**	You wouldn't do that,	**would you?**
They can hear me,	**can't they?**	He can't speak Japanese,	**can he?**

Be careful!
Use <u>aren't I?</u> for negative tag questions
after <u>I am.</u>
   I'm on time, **aren't I?** BUT I'm not late, **am I?**
Use pronouns, not names or other nouns,
in tag questions.
   Bangkok is in Thailand, isn't **it?**
   NOT ~~isn't Bangkok?~~

GRAMMAR BOOSTER ▸ p. 122

• *Tag questions: short answers*

A Find the grammar Find a tag question in the Photo Story on page 3.

B Grammar practice Complete each statement with a tag question.

1 Rob is your manager, ...?

2 I turned off the projector, ...?

3 Tim is going to present next, ...?

4 She won't be at the meeting before 2:00, ...?

5 We haven't forgotten anything, ...?

6 There was no one here from China, ...?

7 The agenda can't be printed in the business center before 8:00 A.M., ...?

8 They were explaining the etiquette rules, ...?

9 She wants to be addressed by her first name, ...?

10 It was a great day, ...?

1:06

A 🔊 Rising intonation usually indicates that the speaker is confirming the correctness of information. Read and listen. Then listen again and repeat.

1 People use first names here, don't they?

2 That meeting was great, wasn't it?

3 It's a beautiful day for a walk, isn't it?

1:07

B 🔊 Falling intonation usually indicates that the speaker expects the listener to agree. Read and listen. Then listen again and repeat.

1 People use first names here, don't they?

2 That meeting was great, wasn't it?

3 It's a beautiful day for a walk, isn't it?

C Pair work Take turns reading the examples of tag questions in the grammar chart on page 4. Read each with both rising and falling intonation.

NOW YOU CAN Make small talk

A Pair work Change the Conversation Model to greet a classmate. Make small talk. Ask each other about how you would like to be addressed. Then change partners.

A: Good ...., isn't it?

B: It really is. By the way, I'm ....

A: I'm ....

Ideas for tag questions
• [Awful] weather, ...
• Nice [afternoon], ...
• Great [English class], ...
• [Good] food, ...
• The food is [terrible], ...

Don't stop!
• Continue making small talk.
• Get to know your new classmates.
• Ask about families, jobs, travel, etc.

B Extension Write your name and a few facts about yourself on a sheet of paper and put it on a table. Choose another classmate's paper, read it quickly, and put it back on the table. Then meet that person and confirm the information you read, using tag questions.

Maria Carbone

I grew up here, but my parents are from

Italy. I started studying English when I was

in primary school.

❝ Maria, hi! I'm Deborah. Your parents are from Italy, aren't they? ❞

GOAL **Describe a busy schedule**

GRAMMAR   *The past perfect: meaning, form, and use*

Use the past perfect to describe an action that happened (or didn't happen) before another action or before a specific time in the past.

Our flight **had arrived** by noon.
The meeting **hadn't** yet **begun** when we arrived.

Past perfect form: <u>had</u> + past participle

Use the past perfect with the simple past tense to clarify which of two past events occurred first.

The meeting **had ended** late, so we had a short lunch.
    (First action: The meeting ended; later action: we had lunch.)
When the tour **started**, Ann **had** already **met** Kazuko.
    (First action: Ann and Kazuko met; later action: the tour started.)

Note: In informal speech, it's common to use the simple past tense instead of the past perfect. The words <u>by</u>, <u>before</u>, and <u>after</u> often clarify the order of the events.

By April, he **started** his new job.
Before I got married, I **got** a degree in marketing.
After I learned to make presentations, they **promoted** me.

GRAMMAR BOOSTER ▸ p. 123

• *Verb usage: present and past (review)*

A Grammar practice Choose the correct meaning for each statement.

1 "Before they decided to have the meeting in Bangkok, I had already decided to take my vacation there."
   ☐ First they decided to have the meeting in Bangkok. Then I decided to take my vacation there.
   ☐ First I decided to take my vacation in Bangkok. Then they decided to have the meeting there.

2 "By the time she got to the meeting, she had already reviewed the agenda."
   ☐ First she reviewed the agenda. Then she got to the meeting.
   ☐ First she got to the meeting. Then she reviewed the agenda.

3 "They had already asked us to turn off our cell phones when the CEO began her presentation."
   ☐ First they asked us to turn off our cell phones. Then the CEO began her presentation.
   ☐ First the CEO began her presentation. Then they asked us to turn off our cell phones.

4 "I had changed into business casual dress before the meeting started."
   ☐ First the meeting started. Then I changed into business casual dress.
   ☐ First I changed into business casual dress. Then the meeting started.

B Meg Ash has to travel to a sales meeting in Seoul tomorrow. It's now 7:00 P.M. Read her to-do list and complete the statements, using <u>already</u> or <u>yet</u>.

1 At 8:30 Meg .... her laundry, but she .... the cat to her mom's house.

2 By 10:45 she .... the cat to her mom's house, but she .... for the meeting.

3 By 12:15 she .... the sales binders at Office Plus, but she .... lunch with Adam.

4 At 1:30 she .... lunch with Adam, but she .... the DVDs to FilmPix.

5 By 2:15 she .... the DVDs to FilmPix, but she .... the dentist.

6 At 5:55 she .... the dentist, but she .... a manicure.

Monday, January 4

8:00	Drop off the laundry at Minute Wash.
9:00	
10:00	Take the cat to Mom's house.
11:00	Pack for the meeting.
12:00	Pick up the sales binders at Office Plus.
1:00	Lunch with Adam
2:00	Return the DVDs to FilmPix.
3:00	
4:00	See dentist. ☹
5:00	5:30 Pick up the laundry from Minute Wash.
6:00	Get a manicure if there's time!
7:00	
8:00	

1:08

A 🔊 Read and listen to someone describing a busy schedule.

A: So how was your day?

B: <u>Unbelievably</u> busy. By 9:00 I had already taken the placement test, registered for class, and bought my books.

A: That's a lot to do before 9:00!

B: That was nothing. At 10:00 I had to be across town for a meeting.

A: Wow!

B: And then I had to get back for the class at 1:00.

A: What did you do about lunch?

B: Well, when I got to class, I hadn't eaten yet, so I just got a snack.

A: You must be <u>pretty</u> hungry by now!

1:10

🔊 **Intensifiers**

+++ unbelievably
+++ incredibly
++ really
++ so
+ pretty

1:09

B 🔊 **Rhythm and intonation** Listen again and repeat. Then practice the Conversation Model with a partner.

NOW YOU CAN | Describe a busy schedule

A Pair work Change the Conversation Model to describe a busy day, morning, afternoon, evening, week, or any other period of time in the past. Then change roles.

A: So how was your ....?

B: .... busy. By .... I .... already ....

A: That's a lot to do before ....!

B: That was nothing. ....

A: Wow!

B: And then I ....

A: What did you do about ....?

B: ....

A: You must be ....!

Don't stop!
• Ask more questions about your partner's activities.
• Provide more details about the activities.

B Change partners Practice the conversation again. Ask other classmates to describe their busy schedules.

7

GOAL **Develop your cultural awareness**

BEFORE YOU LISTEN

A 🔊 1:11 **Vocabulary • *Manners and etiquette*** Read and listen. Then listen again and repeat.

etiquette the "rules" for polite behavior in society or in a particular group

cultural literacy knowing about and respecting the culture of others

table manners rules for polite behavior when eating with other people

punctuality the habit of being on time

impolite not polite, rude

offensive extremely rude or impolite

customary usual or traditional in a particular culture

taboo not allowed because of very strong cultural or religious rules

B Complete each sentence with the correct word or phrase from the Vocabulary.

1 It's (taboo / impolite) to eat pork in some religions. No one would ever do it.

2 Many people believe that (cultural literacy / punctuality) is important and that being late is impolite.

3 In some cultures, it's (offensive / customary) to take pictures of people without permission, so few people do that.

4 Some people think that talking with a mouth full of food is an example of bad (cultural literacy / table manners).

5 In some cultures, it's (customary / offensive) to name children after a living relative, and most people observe that tradition.

6 Each culture has rules of (cultural literacy / etiquette) that are important for visitors to that country to know.

7 In more conservative cultures, it's slightly (impolite / taboo) to call someone by his or her first name without being invited, but it isn't truly offensive.

8 The most successful global travelers today have developed their (punctuality / cultural literacy) so they are aware of differences in etiquette from culture to culture.

Some people eat with a fork, some with chopsticks, and some with their hands.

C **Discussion** Discuss your opinions, using the Vocabulary.

1 What are some good ways to teach children etiquette? Give examples.

2 Do you know of any differences in etiquette between your culture and others? Give examples.

3 Why are table manners important in almost all cultures? How would people behave if there were no rules?

LISTENING COMPREHENSION

A 🔊 1:12 **Listen for main ideas** Look at the subjects on the chart. Listen to three calls from a radio show. Check the subjects that are discussed during each call.

B 🔊 1:13 **Summarize** Listen again. On a separate sheet of paper, take notes about the calls. Then, with a partner, write a summary of each call. Use the Vocabulary.

Subjects	1 Arturo / Jettrin	2 Hiroko / Nadia	3 Javier / Sujeet
table manners	☐	☐	☐
greetings	☐	☐	☐
dress and clothing	☐	☐	☐
male / female behavior	☐	☐	☐
taboos	☐	☐	☐
offensive behavior	☐	☐	☐
punctuality	☐	☐	☐
language	☐	☐	☐

A Frame your ideas With a partner, look at the questions about your culture on the notepad. Discuss each question and write your answers to the questions.

How do people greet each other when they meet for the first time?

How do they greet each other when they already know each other?

Are greeting customs different for men and women? How?

When and how do you address people formally?

When and how do you address people informally?

What are some do's and don'ts for table manners?

Are certain foods or beverages taboo?

What are some taboo conversation topics?

What are the customs about punctuality?

What is a customary gift if you are visiting someone's home?

Are there any gift taboos (kinds of flowers, etc.)?

Are there places where certain clothes would be inappropriate?

Is there an important aspect of your culture that's not on this list?

C Group work Role-play a conversation with a visitor to your country. Tell the visitor about your culture. Use the answers to the questions on the notepad.

" It's bad table manners to pick up a soup bowl and drink soup from it. You have to use a spoon. "

" It's not customary for a man to extend his hand to shake hands with a woman. He should wait for the woman to do that. "

B Discussion Combine classmates' notes on the board for the class to share. Does everyone agree? Discuss your differences of opinion.

BEFORE YOU READ

A Use prior knowledge In what ways do you think table manners have changed since the days when your grandparents were children?

B Predict the topic Look at the title of the article, the original date of publication, and the internal headings. Use those cues to predict what the article will be about.

READING 1:14

Formal Dinner Etiquette

It is very discourteous for a guest to be late. Arrive at least five minutes before the hour set for the dinner. If for some unavoidable reason you cannot arrive on time, telephone the hostess and explain the reason to her. Etiquette only requires that she wait for fifteen minutes before beginning the meal. If it has been impossible for you to notify her and she has started the meal, go to her, offer apologies, and take your place at the table as quickly as possible.

SEATING

The hostess leads the female guests into the dining room. The host and the male guests follow. The hostess then tells her guests where to sit. She must always have the seating arrangement planned in advance in order to avoid confusion and delay.

Each person stands casually behind his chair until the hostess starts to take her seat. The man helps his dinner partner to be seated and also helps move her chair as she rises. Each person moves to the left of the chair to be seated and also rises from the left.

Originally published in 1940 in the United States

THE MEAL

At a small dinner party, do not start to eat until all guests are served. At a large dinner party, you may start to eat as soon as those near you have been served. Do not eat too fast. Do not talk while you have food in your mouth, and keep the mouth closed while you chew your food. Elbows should not be put on the table when you are eating (however, between courses at a restaurant, if you cannot hear your companion, it is permissible to lean forward on your elbows).

If silver is dropped on the floor, leave it there. If an accident happens at the table, apologize briefly to your hostess.

The hostess continues to eat as long as her guests do. When all have finished, she rises from the table and the others follow.

DEPARTING

If you have no dinner partner, push your chair from the table by taking hold of each side of the seat of the chair. Don't rest your hands or arms on the table to push yourself up.

It is not necessary to remain longer than thirty minutes after a dinner if the invitation does not include the entire evening. However, one should avoid appearing in a hurry to leave.

Source: www.Oldandsold.com

A Confirm facts On a separate sheet of paper, answer the questions about dinner party etiquette in the 1940s.

1 If the dinner party invitation is for 8:00, what time should guests arrive?

> *Guests should arrive by 7:55 at the latest.*

2 If a guest is going to be late, what should he or she do?

3 Who decides where guests should sit at the table?

4 What are the different roles or expectations of men and women at a dinner party?

5 When should a guest begin eating?

6 What should a guest do if a fork or a knife falls to the floor?

7 What should a guest do if he or she spills a drink on the table?

8 How long should the host or hostess continue eating?

9 What should a guest do when the host or hostess leaves the table?

10 How long should guests stay after dinner is over?

B Summarize Summarize how dinner party etiquette has changed since the 1940s. Use the questions in Exercise A on page 10 as a guide.

On your *ActiveBook* Self-Study Disc:
Extra Reading Comprehension Questions

NOW YOU CAN   Discuss how culture changes over time

A Frame your ideas Think about how culture has changed since your grandparents were your age. Complete the survey.

Culture Survey

	have changed a little	have changed a lot	Is the change for the better? (YES or NO)	
1. Table manners	☐	☐	☐	☐
2. Musical tastes	☐	☐	☐	☐
3. Dating customs	☐	☐	☐	☐
4. Clothing customs	☐	☐	☐	☐
5. Rules about formal behavior	☐	☐	☐	☐
6. Rules about punctuality	☐	☐	☐	☐
7. Forms of address	☐	☐	☐	☐
8. Male / female roles in the workplace	☐	☐	☐	☐
9. Male / female roles in the home	☐	☐	☐	☐

Total YES answers: _____

Are you a dinosaur or a chameleon?

How many times did you check YES in the third column?

0–3 = Definitely a dinosaur. You prefer to stick with tradition. Your motto: "If it isn't broken, don't fix it!"

4–6 = A little of both. You're willing to adapt to change, but not too fast. Your motto: "Easy does it!"

7–9 = Definitely a chameleon. You adapt to change easily. Your motto: "Out with the old, in with the new!"

B Pair work Compare and discuss your answers. Provide specific examples of changes for each answer. Use the past perfect if you can.

> "I think clothing customs have become less modest. My mother had to wear a uniform to school. But by the time I started school, girls had stopped wearing them. Now girls can go to school in jeans and even shorts!"

C Discussion Talk about how culture has changed. Include these topics in your discussion:

- Which changes do you think are good? Which changes are not good? Explain your reasons.
- How do you think older people feel about these changes?
- Do you think men and women differ in their feelings about cultural change? If so, how?

♻ **Be sure to recycle this language.**

Formality	Tag questions	Agreement / Disagreement
be on a first-name basis	[People don't ___ as much], do they?	I agree.
prefer to be addressed by ___	[Customs used to be ___], didn't they?	I think you're right.
It's impolite to ___ .		I disagree.
It's offensive to ___ .		Actually, I don't agree because ___ .
It's customary to ___ .		Really? I think ___ .
It isn't customary to ___ .		

Review

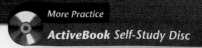

More Practice

ActiveBook *Self-Study Disc*

grammar · vocabulary · listening
reading · speaking · pronunciation

A ◀)) **Listening comprehension** Listen to the conversations between
people introducing themselves. Check the statement that correctly
paraphrases the main idea.

1. ☐ She'd like to be addressed by her title and family name.
   ☐ She'd like to be addressed by her first name.

2. ☐ She'd prefer to be called by her first name.
   ☐ She'd prefer to be called by her title and last name.

3. ☐ It's customary to call people by their first name there.
   ☐ It's not customary to call people by their first name there.

4. ☐ He's comfortable with the policy about names.
   ☐ He's not comfortable with the policy about names.

5. ☐ She prefers to use the title "Mrs."
   ☐ She prefers to use the title "Dr."

> 1:16 / 1:17
> ♫ **Top Notch Pop**
> "It's a Great Day for Love"
> Lyrics p. 149

B Complete each sentence with a tag question.

1. You're not from around here, ...?

2. You were in this class last year, ...?

3. They haven't been here since yesterday, ...?

4. Before the class, she hadn't yet told them how she wanted to be addressed, ...?

5. I can bring flowers as a gift for the hosts, ...?

6. You won't be back in time for dinner, ...?

7. I met you on the tour in Nepal, ...?

8. We'll have a chance to discuss this tomorrow, ...?

9. They were going to dinner, ...?

10. My friends are going to be surprised to see you, ...?

C Complete each statement with the correct word or phrase.

1. Offending other people when eating a meal is an example of bad ....

2. Each country has customs and traditions about how to behave in social situations.
   The rules are sometimes called ....

3. Each culture has its own sense of .... It's important to
   understand people's ideas about lateness.

D Writing On a separate sheet of paper, write two e-mail messages—one
formal and one informal—telling someone about the cultural traditions in
your country. Review the questionnaire about cultural traditions on
page 9 for information to select from.

> **WRITING BOOSTER** ▸ p. 141
> • Formal e-mail etiquette
> • Guidance for Exercise D

• For the formal e-mail, imagine you are writing to a businessperson who
  is coming to your country on a business trip.

• For the informal e-mail, imagine you are writing to a friend who is
  visiting your country as a tourist.

Tell a story First, look at the pictures and tell the story of the Garzas and the Itos on June 10. Then, look at the itineraries below and use the past perfect to talk about what they had done by June 5. Start like this:

By June 5, the Itos had been to . . .

Pair work Create conversations.
1 Create a conversation for the two men in the first picture. Each man tells the other how he'd like to be addressed.
2 Create a conversation for the two women in the second picture. The women are making small talk.
3 Create a conversation for the people in the third picture. Ask and answer questions about the their trips to Peru. Use the past perfect when possible.

JUNE 10, 10:00A.M.

María and Antonio Garza

Haru and Kimi Ito

LATER THAT DAY

GLOBAL ADVENTURES, INC.

Haru and Kimi Ito–Peru Itinerary

May 29
Lima: María Angola Hotel
La Paz 610, Miraflores

May 31
Puno: Casa Andina Classic
Jr. Independencia 185, Plaza de Armas

June 4
Cusco: Novotel
San Agustín 239

June 9
Machu Picchu: Hanaq Pacha Hotel
(Aguas Calientes)

GetAway Travel, Inc.

María and Antonio Garza—
Peru itinerary

May 30
Lima: María Angola Hotel
La Paz 610, Miraflores

June 3
Arequipa: Tierra Sur Hotel
Consuelo 210

June 6
Nasca: Brabant Hostel
Calle Juan Matta 978

June 9
Machu Picchu: Hanaq Pacha Hotel
(Aguas Calientes)

NOW I CAN... ✓

☐ Make small talk.
☐ Describe a busy schedule.
☐ Develop cultural awareness.
☐ Discuss how culture changes over time.

Health Matters

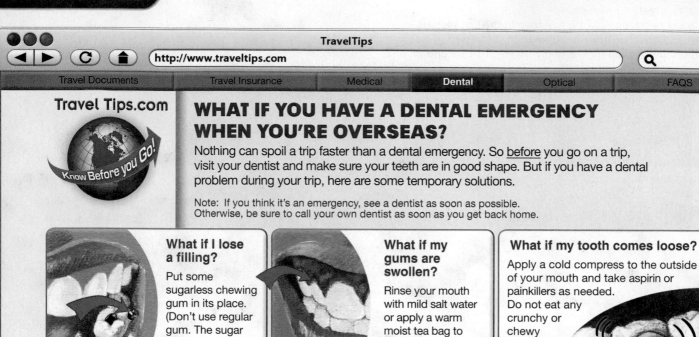

TravelTips

http://www.traveltips.com

| Travel Documents | Travel Insurance | Medical | **Dental** | Optical | FAQS |

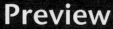

Travel Tips.com
Know Before you Go!

WHAT IF YOU HAVE A DENTAL EMERGENCY WHEN YOU'RE OVERSEAS?

Nothing can spoil a trip faster than a dental emergency. So <u>before</u> you go on a trip, visit your dentist and make sure your teeth are in good shape. But if you have a dental problem during your trip, here are some temporary solutions.

Note: If you think it's an emergency, see a dentist as soon as possible. Otherwise, be sure to call your own dentist as soon as you get back home.

What if I lose a filling?

Put some sugarless chewing gum in its place. (Don't use regular gum. The sugar will hurt!)

more

What if my gums are swollen?

Rinse your mouth with mild salt water or apply a warm moist tea bag to the gums.

more

What if my tooth comes loose?

Apply a cold compress to the outside of your mouth and take aspirin or painkillers as needed. Do not eat any crunchy or chewy foods.

more

What if I break a tooth?

Depending on how much of your tooth has broken off, you may be able to wait till you return home to see your dentist. If you feel any pain, apply a washcloth dipped in very cold water to the outside of the mouth and take aspirin or another painkiller.

more

What if I have a lot of tooth pain?

If you have a toothache, rinse your mouth with warm water and put a cold compress against your cheek. In some cases, flying in a plane can make a toothache worse, so make sure you have aspirin or another painkiller with you.

more

Information source: www.webmd.com

A Discussion Do you think the information in the website is useful? Why do you think some people would wait until they got back home to see a dentist?

B Pair work Discuss each of the situations described in the website and what you would do. Circle <u>yes</u> or <u>no</u>.

I would . . .		
• ignore the problem.	yes	no
• make an appointment to see a dentist right away.	yes	no
• call or e-mail my own dentist and ask for advice.	yes	no
• use the remedy suggested in the website.	yes	no
• use my own remedy (explain).	yes	no

C 🔊 1:18 **Photo story** Read and listen to someone with a dental emergency during a trip.

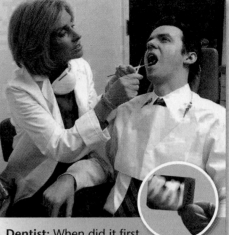

Guest: I need to see a dentist as soon as possible. I think it's an emergency. I was wondering if you might be able to recommend someone who speaks English.

Clerk: Let me check. Actually, there is one not far from here. Would you like me to make an appointment for you?

Guest: If you could. Thanks. I'm in a lot of pain.

Dentist: So I hear you're from overseas.

Patient: From Ecuador. Thanks for fitting me in.

Dentist: Luckily, I had a cancellation. So what brings you in today?

Patient: Well, this tooth is killing me.

Dentist: When did it first begin to hurt?

Patient: It's been bothering me since last night.

Dentist: Let's have a look. Open wide.

Patient: Ah . . .

Dentist: Well, let's take an X-ray and see what's going on.

Guest (Patient): Spanish speaker / Clerk and dentist: Russian speakers

D **Focus on language** Find the underlined statements in the Photo Story. Then use the context to help you restate each one in your own words.

1 I was wondering if you might be able to recommend someone who speaks English.

2 If you could. Thanks.

3 Thanks for fitting me in.

4 This tooth is killing me.

5 It's been bothering me since last night.

6 Let's have a look.

7 Let's take an X-ray and see what's going on.

E **Personalize** Have you—or has someone you know—ever had an emergency that required dental or medical attention? Complete the chart.

Where did it happen?	When did it happen?	What happened?

F **Group work** Tell your classmates about your emergency.

> ❝ Last year, I went skiing and I broke my arm. I had to go to the emergency room at the hospital. ❞

GOAL **Call in sick**

VOCABULARY *Symptoms*

A 🔊 1:19 Read and listen. Then listen again and repeat.

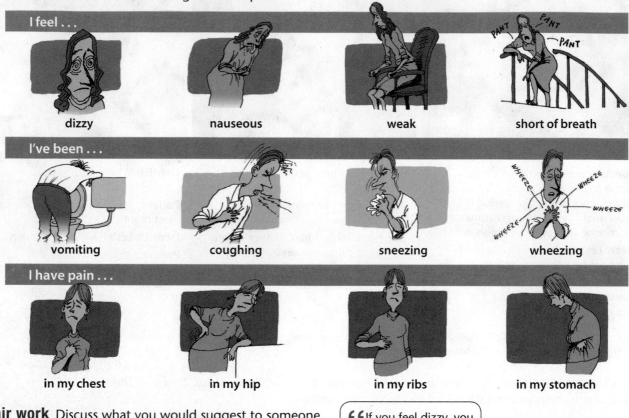

I feel . . .

dizzy   nauseous   weak   short of breath

I've been . . .

vomiting   coughing   sneezing   wheezing

I have pain . . .

in my chest   in my hip   in my ribs   in my stomach

B **Pair work** Discuss what you would suggest to someone with some of the symptoms in the Vocabulary.

> "If you feel dizzy, you should lie down."

C 🔊 1:20 **Listening comprehension** Listen and check the symptoms each patient describes. Then listen again. If the patient has pain, write where it is.

	dizziness	nausea	weakness	vomiting	coughing	sneezing	wheezing	pain	If pain, where?
1	☐	☐	☐	☐	☐	☐	☐	☐	
2	☐	☐	☐	☐	☐	☐	☐	☐	
3	☐	☐	☐	☐	☐	☐	☐	☐	
4	☐	☐	☐	☐	☐	☐	☐	☐	
5	☐	☐	☐	☐	☐	☐	☐	☐	
6	☐	☐	☐	☐	☐	☐	☐	☐	

PRONUNCIATION *Intonation of lists*

A 🔊 1:21 Use rising intonation on each item before the last item in a list. Use falling intonation on the last item. Read and listen. Then listen again and repeat.

1 I feel weak and dizzy.

2 I've been sneezing, coughing, and wheezing.

3 I have pain in my neck, my shoulders, my back, and my hip.

B Pair work Take turns using the Vocabulary to make lists of symptoms. Practice correct intonation for lists.

> ❝I feel dizzy, weak, and short of breath.❞

GRAMMAR Modal *must*: drawing conclusions

> Use **must** and the base form of a verb to indicate that you think something is probably true.
> A: I think I just broke my tooth!
> B: Oh, no. That **must hurt**.
>
> A: The doctor said I should come in next week.
> B: Oh, good. It **must not be** an emergency.

GRAMMAR BOOSTER ▸ p. 124
• Other ways to draw conclusions: <u>probably</u>; <u>most likely</u>

Grammar practice Complete the conversations by drawing conclusions, using <u>must</u> or <u>must not</u>.

1 A: You look awful! You .... in a lot of pain.
   _{be}

   B: I am.

2 A: Gary just called. He has a bad headache.

   B: Too bad. He .... to go running.
   _{want}

3 A: My doctor says I'm in perfect health.

   B: That's great. You .... really good.
   _{feel}

4 A: Did you call the dentist?

   B: Yes, I did. But no one's answering. She .... in today.
   _{be}

CONVERSATION MODEL

A 🔊 1:22 Read and listen to someone calling in sick.

   A: I'm afraid I'm not going to be able to come in today.

   B: I'm sorry to hear that. Is something wrong?

   A: Actually, I'm not feeling too well. I've been coughing and wheezing for a couple of days.

   B: That must be awful. Maybe you should see a doctor.

   A: I think I will.

   B: Good. Call me tomorrow and let me know how you feel. OK?

B 🔊 1:23 **Rhythm and intonation** Listen again and repeat. Then practice the Conversation Model with a partner.

NOW YOU CAN Call in sick

A Pair work Change the Conversation Model to describe other symptoms. Use <u>must</u> or must <u>not</u> to draw conclusions. Then change roles.

   A: I'm afraid I'm not going to be able to .... today.

   B: .... Is something wrong?

   A: Actually, I'm not feeling too well. I ....

   B: That must be .... Maybe you should ....

   A: ....

   B: .... Call me tomorrow and let me know how you feel. OK?

B Change partners Call in sick for other situations such as school or social events.

Don't stop!
• Ask more questions about your partner's symptoms.
• Give your partner more suggestions about what to do.

♻ **Be sure to recycle this language.**

Ask questions
Are you [coughing]?
Did you try ___?
Make suggestions
You should / You'd better ___.
Why don't you try ___?
How about ___?
Draw conclusions
You must feel awful / terrible.
That must hurt.

GOAL **Make a medical or dental appointment**

GRAMMAR *Will be able to; Modals may and might*

Will be able to + base form: future ability
The doctor **will be able to see** you tomorrow. (= The doctor can see you tomorrow.)
She'**ll be able to play** tennis again in a week or so. (= She can play tennis again in a week or so.)

May or might + base form: possibility
The dentist **might have** some time to see you this afternoon.
You **may need** to come in right away.

Note: You can use be able to with may and might for possibility or with must for drawing conclusions.

The doctor	**may be able to**	**see** you today.
I	**might not be able to**	**get** there till 6:00.
We	**must be able to**	**park** here—see the sign?
They	**must not be able to**	**cancel** the appointment.

GRAMMAR BOOSTER ▸ p. 125

• *Expressing possibility with maybe*

Grammar practice Complete each conversation. Use <u>may/might</u>, <u>may/might be able to</u>, or <u>must not be able to</u> and the base form.

1 A: I'd like to see a dentist right away. I think it's an emergency.

B: Well, I .... you an
get
appointment at 2:00. Would that be OK?

2 A: Is Dr. Lindt in this morning? I'm not feeling very well.

B: She is, but she doesn't have any openings. However, she .... time to see you this afternoon.have

3 A: I think I .... allergic to
be
strawberries. I had some for breakfast, and I have a rash all over my body.

B: Then you'd better come in this morning.
I .... you in right
before noon.fit

4 A: I've been calling Mr. Reis for an hour. I know he's home, but no one's answering.

B: That's strange. He ....
the phone.hear

VOCABULARY *Medical procedures*

A 🔊 1:24 Read and listen. Then listen again and repeat.

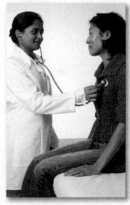
a checkup /
an examination

a shot /
an injection

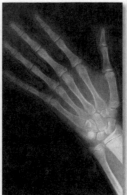
an EKG /
an electrocardiogram

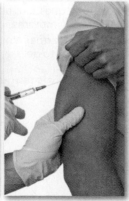
an X-ray

a blood test

B **Pair work** Discuss when a person might need each medical procedure from the Vocabulary.

> " If you have pain in your arm, you might need an X-ray. "

1:25

A 🔊 Read and listen to someone making an appointment.

A: Hello. Doctor Star's office. Can I help you?

B: Hello. I need to make an appointment for a blood test. I wonder if I might be able to come in early next week.

A: Let's see if I can fit you in. How about Tuesday?

B: Could I come in the morning?

A: Let me check . . . Would you be able to be here at 10:00?

B: That would be perfect.

A: We'll see you then.

B: Thanks! I really appreciate it.

1:26

B 🔊 **Rhythm and intonation** Listen again and repeat. Then practice the Conversation Model with a partner.

NOW YOU CAN Make a medical or dental appointment

A **Pair work** Make an appointment to see a doctor or dentist. Suggest a day. Write the appointment on the schedule. Then change roles.

A: Hello. Doctor .... 's office. Can I help you?

B: Hello. I need to make an appointment for .... I wonder if I might be able to come in ....

A: Let's see if I can fit you in. Would you be able to be here at .... ?

B: ....

Don't stop!
• Say you can't be there today.
• Discuss other days and times.

Ideas
• tomorrow
• next week
• early next week
• at the end of next week
• the week of [the 3rd]

B **Change partners** Make another appointment.

	Patient's name	Medical procedure
8:00	Bill Reed	blood test
9:00	Maria Patton	chest X-ray
10:00		
11:00		
12:00		
1:00	Angela Baker	checkup
2:00	Victor Gaines	flu shot
3:00		
4:00	Teresa Keyes	EKG
5:00		
6:00	Anna Holmes	chest X-ray
7:00		
8:00		
9:00		
10:00		

19

GOAL **Discuss types of treatments**

BEFORE YOU READ

Warm-up What do you do when you get sick or you're in pain? Do you treat the problem yourself or see a doctor right away?

READING 1:27

Consider the choices . . .

CONVENTIONAL MEDICINE

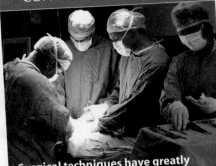

Surgical techniques have greatly improved over the last century.

The beginnings of conventional medicine can be traced back to the fifth century B.C.E. in ancient Greece. It is based on the scientific study of the human body and illness.

In the last century, there has been great progress in what doctors have been able to do with modern surgery and new medications. These scientific advances have made conventional medicine the method many people choose first when they need medical treatment.

HOMEOPATHY

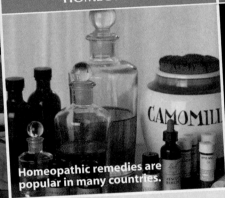

Homeopathic remedies are popular in many countries.

Homeopathy was founded in the late eighteenth century in Germany. It is a low-cost system of natural medicine used by hundreds of millions of people worldwide.

In homeopathy, a patient's symptoms are treated with remedies that cause similar symptoms. The remedy is taken in very diluted form: 1 part remedy to one trillion (1,000,000,000,000) parts water.

HERBAL THERAPY

Herbs are used to treat many ailments.

Herbal medicine, often taken as teas or pills, has been practiced for thousands of years in almost all cultures around the world. In fact, many conventional medicines were discovered by scientists studying traditional uses of herbs for medical purposes.

The World Health Organization claims that 80% of the world's population uses some form of herbal therapy for their regular health care.

ACUPUNCTURE

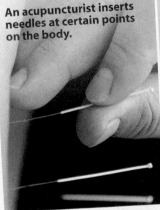

An acupuncturist inserts needles at certain points on the body.

Acupuncture originated in China over 5,000 years ago. Today, it is used worldwide for a variety of problems.

Acupuncture needles are inserted at certain points on the body to relieve pain and/or restore health. Many believe acupuncture may be effective in helping people stop smoking as well.

SPIRITUAL HEALING

Many believe meditation or prayer may help heal disease.

Also known as faith healing, or "mind and body connection," various forms of spiritual healing exist around the world. This is a form of healing that uses the mind or religious faith to treat illness.

A number of conventional doctors say that when they have not been able to help a patient, spiritual healing just may work.

Sources: www.alternativemedicine.com and www.holisticmed.com

A Understand from context
Five of these words have similar meanings.
Cross out the three words that don't belong. Look at the article again for help.

remedy	treatment	therapy	advances
resources	healing	care	purposes

B Relate to personal experience
Talk about the following questions.

1 Which of the treatments in the Reading have you or your family tried?

2 Which treatments do you think are the most effective? Why?

C Draw conclusions
Decide which treatment or treatments each patient would probably NOT want to try and which he or she might prefer. Explain your answers, using <u>might</u> or <u>might not</u>. (More than one therapy might be appropriate.)

1 **"**I definitely want to see a doctor when I have a problem. But I want to avoid taking any strong medications or having surgery.**"**

2 **"**I believe you have to heal yourself. You can't just expect a doctor to do everything for you.**"**

3 **"**I think it would be crazy to try a health care method that isn't strongly supported by scientific research.**"**

On your *ActiveBook* Self-Study Disc:
Extra Reading Comprehension Questions

NOW YOU CAN Discuss types of treatments

A Notepadding
With a partner, discuss treatments you would choose for each ailment. What kind of practitioner would you visit? Complete your notepad.

Practitioners
- a conventional doctor
- a homeopathic doctor
- an acupuncturist
- an herbal therapist
- a spiritual healer

Ailment	You	Your partner
a cold		
a headache		
nausea		
back pain		
a high fever		
a broken finger		

B Discussion
Compare the kinds of treatments you and your classmates would use. Say what you learned about your partner.

"I would never try herbal therapy. I just don't think it works. My partner agrees.**"**

"My partner has been to an acupuncturist a number of times. It really helped with her back pain.**"**

"I see a homeopathic doctor regularly, but my partner doesn't believe in that. He prefers a conventional doctor.**"**

GOAL **Talk about medications**

Medicine label information
Dosage: Take 1 tablet by mouth every day.
Warnings: Do not take while driving or operating machinery.
Side effects: May cause dizziness or nausea.

BEFORE YOU LISTEN

A 🔊 **Vocabulary • *Medications*** Read and listen.
Then listen again and repeat.

1:28

a prescription

a painkiller

cold tablets

**a nasal spray /
a decongestant**

eye drops

an antihistamine

cough medicine

an antibiotic

an antacid

an ointment

vitamins

B **Pair work** Discuss what you might use
each medication for.

❝I might take an antacid
for a stomachache.❞

LISTENING COMPREHENSION

A 🔊 **Listen for key details** Listen to each conversation with a doctor.
Use the medications Vocabulary above and the symptoms Vocabulary from
page 16 to complete the chart for each patient.

1:30

Name: _Didem Yilmaz_
What are the patient's symptoms?

Is the patient currently taking any
medications? ☐ Yes ☐ No

If so, which ones?

Did the patient get a prescription?
☐ Yes ☐ No

Name: _Lucy Fernández_
What are the patient's symptoms?

Is the patient currently taking any
medications? ☐ Yes ☐ No
If so, which ones?

Did the patient get a prescription?
☐ Yes ☐ No

Name: _Mark Goh_
What are the patient's symptoms?

Is the patient currently taking any
medications? ☐ Yes ☐ No
If so, which ones?

Did the patient get a prescription?
☐ Yes ☐ No

B 🔊 1:31 **Listen for more details** Listen again. Complete the information about each patient.

Mark Goh
Dosage: Apply ointment _____ a day
Side effects: ☐ Yes ☐ No
If so, what are they? _____
_____
_____

Didem Yilmaz
Dosage: One tablet _____ a day
Side effects: ☐ Yes ☐ No
If so, what are they? _____
_____
_____

Lucy Fernández
Dosage: _____ a day
Side effects: ☐ Yes ☐ No
If so, what are they? _____
_____
_____

NOW YOU CAN | Talk about medications

A Preparation Imagine you are visiting the doctor. Complete the patient information form.

B Group work With three other classmates, role-play a visit to a doctor. First, choose roles. Then role-play the three scenes below. Use the patient information form.

Roles
• a patient
• a friend, colleague, classmate, or relative
• a receptionist
• a doctor

Scene 1: The colleague, classmate, friend, or relative recommends a doctor.
Scene 2: The patient calls the receptionist to make an appointment.
Scene 3: The doctor asks about the symptoms and recommends medication, etc.

Patient Information Form

Last name	First name

1. What are your symptoms?
☐ dizziness ☐ coughing ☐ nausea ☐ weakness
☐ sneezing ☐ vomiting ☐ shortness of breath
☐ wheezing ☐ pain (where?)
☐ other:

2. How long have you had these symptoms?

3. Are you currently taking any medications? ☐ Yes ☐ No
If so, which ones?

4. Are you allergic to any medications? ☐ Yes ☐ No
If so, which ones?

♻ **Be sure to recycle this language.**

Scene 1
I've been [wheezing / coughing / dizzy].
I'm in a lot of pain.
Could you recommend ___ ?
I think you should try ___ .
Why don't you ___ ?
You may have to ___ .
I hope you feel better soon.

Scene 2
I need to make an appointment for ___ .
I wonder if I might be able to ___ .
Let me check.
Let's see if I can fit you in.
Would you be able to be here ___ ?
I really appreciate it.

Scene 3
Thanks for fitting me in.
Luckily, I had a cancellation.
Let's have a look.
Are you taking any medications?
Are you allergic to any medications?
Are there any side effects?
Call me tomorrow.

C Presentation Perform your role play for the class.

Review

More Practice

ActiveBook *Self-Study Disc*

grammar · vocabulary · listening
reading · speaking · pronunciation

A ◀)) **Listening comprehension** Listen to each conversation and complete the statements. Then listen again to check your answers.

The patient lost .... when she was eating ....

The patient has .... She needs to take ....

The patient needs .... of his ....

The patient would like to try .... for pain in her ....

B Suggest a medication for each person. (Answers will vary.)

1 ....

2 ....

3 ....

4 ....

5 ....

C Complete each conversation by drawing your own conclusion with <u>must</u>.

1 A: I feel really nauseous. I've been vomiting all morning.

B: You *must feel terrible* ....

2 A: My dentist can't fit me in till next month.

B: Your dentist ....

3 A: My daughter was sick, but it wasn't anything serious, thank goodness.

B: You ....

4 A: My husband fell down and broke his ankle.

B: He .... !

D On a separate sheet of paper, rewrite each statement, using <u>may</u> (or <u>might</u>) and <u>be able to</u>.

1 Maybe the doctor can see you tomorrow.

2 Maybe an acupuncturist can help you.

3 Maybe the hotel can recommend a good dentist.

4 Maybe she can't come to the office before 6:00.

5 Maybe you can buy an antihistamine in the hotel gift shop.

> *The doctor might be able to see you tomorrow.*

E **Writing** On a separate sheet of paper, compare two types of medical treatments. Use the Reading on page 20 and your own experiences and ideas. Consider the following questions:

• How are the two medical treatments similar or different?

• Which treatment do you think is more effective?

• Why might people choose each treatment?

• Which treatments do you—or people you know—use? Why?

1:33/1:34

♪ *Top Notch Pop*
"X-ray of My Heart"
Lyrics p. 149

WRITING BOOSTER ▸ p. 141

• *Comparisons and contrasts*
• *Guidance for Exercise E*

Pair work

1 Create a conversation for the people in the photos to the left. Start like this:

I'm afraid I'm not going to be able to come in today. I . . .

2 Create a conversation for the man on the phone and the receptionist in the doctor's office below. Make an appointment. Start like this:

A: *Hello. Can I help you?*
B: *I wonder if I might be able to . . .*

Game Each student takes a turn describing the doctor's office below, using <u>must</u> or <u>may</u> and <u>might</u>. (If a student can't say anything, he or she is out.) For example:

He's touching his arm. He must be in a lot of pain.

NOW I CAN...

- [ ] Call in sick.
- [ ] Make a medical or dental appointment.
- [ ] Discuss types of treatments.
- [ ] Talk about medications.

Getting Things Done

GOALS | After Unit 3, you will be able to:

1 Get someone else to do something.
2 Request express service.
3 Evaluate the quality of service.
4 Plan a meeting or social event.

Are you a PROCRASTINATOR?

Take the survey.

1 At the beginning of every week, you ___.
- ☐ a. always make to-do lists for your calendar
- ☐ b. sometimes make to-do lists, but you often forget
- ☐ c. don't bother with planning and just let things happen

2 When you need to buy someone a gift, you ___.
- ☐ a. get something right away
- ☐ b. buy something a few days before you have to give it
- ☐ c. pick something up on the day you have to give it

3 When you have something that's broken, you ___.
- ☐ a. immediately take it in to be repaired
- ☐ b. wait for a convenient time to take it in
- ☐ c. never get around to taking it in

4 When you have a lot of things you need to do, you do ___.
- ☐ a. the hardest things first
- ☐ b. the easiest things first
- ☐ c. anything but what you need to do

5 When you need to get something done in a short amount of time, you ___.
- ☐ a. feel motivated to work even harder
- ☐ b. feel a little nervous, but you get to work
- ☐ c. have a hard time doing it

6 You ___ feel bad when there are things you haven't gotten done yet.
- ☐ a. always
- ☐ b. sometimes
- ☐ c. rarely

Your results

If you answered "c" four or more times:
You are a classic procrastinator! You tend to put things off.

If you answered "b" four or more times:
You are a bit of a procrastinator, but you try to get things done on time.

If you answered "a" four or more times:
You are organized and self-motivated. You never put off what you can get done now.

Source: adapted from www.blogthings.com.

A Pair work Compare responses on the survey with a partner. Does your score accurately describe the kind of person you are? Explain, using examples.

B Discussion Based on the survey questions, what is a procrastinator? What do you think it means to be an "organized and self-motivated" person? What do you think are the advantages of being that type of person?

C 🔊 **Photo story** Read and listen to some customers placing orders at a copy shop.

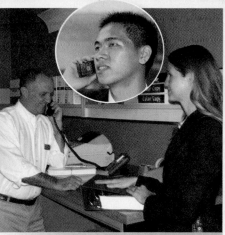

Manager: What can I do for you today, Ms. Krauss?

Customer 1: I need to get these documents copied a.s.a.p.* Think I could get 300 copies done by 11:00?

Manager: I'm afraid that might be difficult. I've got a lot of orders to complete this morning.

Customer 1: Sorry. I know this is last minute. But it's really urgent.

Manager: Well, you're a good customer. Let me see what I can do.

Customer 1: Thanks a million. You're a lifesaver!

Manager: Excuse me . . . Hello. Happy Copy.

Customer 2: Hi, Sam. Ken Li here.

Manager: Hi, Mr. Li. How can I help you today?

Customer 2: Well, I'm going through my to-do list, and I just realized I need to get fifty 30-page sales binders made up for our meeting next week. Any chance I could get them done by first thing tomorrow morning?

Manager: Tomorrow morning? No sweat. Can you get the documents to me before noon?

Customer 2: Absolutely. I owe you one, Sam!

Manager: Sorry to keep you waiting, Ms. Krauss.

Customer 1: Well, I see that you've got a lot on your plate today. I won't keep you any longer.

Manager: Don't worry, Ms. Krauss. We'll get your order done on time.

Customer 1: Should I give you a call later?

Manager: No need for that. Come at 11:00 and I'll have your documents ready.

Customer 1: Thanks, Sam.

*a.s.a.p. = as soon as possible   Customer 2: Chinese speaker

D Paraphrase Say each of the following statements from the Photo Story in your <u>own</u> way.

1 "… this is last minute."

2 "… it's really urgent."

3 "You're a lifesaver!"

4 "No sweat."

5 "I owe you one!"

6 "… you've got a lot on your plate …"

7 "I won't keep you any longer."

E Discussion Based on the survey on page 26, how would you describe each character in the Photo Story? Complete the chart. Then compare charts with your classmates.

	Procrastinator?	Organized?	Explain
Ms. Krauss	☐	☐	
Sam	☐	☐	
Mr. Li	☐	☐	

GOAL	**Get someone else to do something**

GRAMMAR *Causatives get, have, and make*

Use a causative to express the idea that one person causes another to do something.

Get: Use an object and an infinitive.

	object	infinitive
I **got**	**the company**	**to agree** to a new date for the meeting.
They **got**	**the students**	**to clean up** after the party.

Have: Use an object and the base form of a verb.

	object	base form
I **had**	**my assistant**	**plan** the meeting.
They **had**	**the bellman**	**bring** the guests' bags to their rooms.

Make: Use an object and the base form of a verb.

	object	base form
I **made**	**my brother**	**help** me finish the job.
They **made**	**him**	**sign** the form.

> **Causatives: meaning**
> • The causative <u>get</u> implies that someone convinced another person to do something.
> • The causative <u>have</u> implies that instructions were given.
> • The causative <u>make</u> implies an obligation.

GRAMMAR BOOSTER ▸ p. 125

• *Let* to indicate permission
• *Causative have: common errors*

Grammar practice Complete each sentence with a causative.

1 (have / call) Why don't you .... your assistant .... them?

2 (get / do) I'll never be able to .... my brother .... the laundry.

3 (have / clean) Why didn't you .... your friends .... up after the party?

4 (get / give) You should .... the hotel .... you your money back.

5 (make / wash) Why don't you .... your brother .... the dishes?

6 (get / sign) I'm sure we can .... the teacher .... these forms.

VOCABULARY *Some ways to help out another person*

A 🔊 2:03 Read and listen. Then listen again and repeat.

My car's at the repair shop. Could you possibly *give me a ride* to work?

I need to use the men's room. Could you *keep an eye on* my things till I get back?

Excuse me. Would you mind *lending me your pen?*

I can't play soccer this afternoon. You're a good player. Do you think you could *fill in for* me?

I'm too busy to go out for lunch. Do you think you could *pick up* a sandwich for me?

give [someone] **a ride**

keep an eye on [something or someone]

lend [someone] [something]

fill in for [someone]

pick up [something or someone]

B Complete each sentence with one of the verb phrases from the Vocabulary.

1 The meeting doesn't end until 5:00. Do you think you could .... my kids from school at 4:00?

2 Janus usually answers the phones but he's out sick today. Could you possibly .... him?

3 Oops. I'm completely out of cash! Do you think you could .... me some money for lunch?

4 I have to make an important phone call. Could you .... my daughter for about ten minutes?

5 Doris is catching a flight at 9:00. Do you think you might be able to .... her .... to the airport?

CONVERSATION MODEL

A 🔊 2:04 Read and listen to someone asking for a favor.

A: Martin, I wonder if you could do me a favor.

B: Sure. What do you need?

A: My car's at the repair shop and I need to pick it up at 3:00. Do you think you could give me a ride?

B: I would, but I have a doctor's appointment at 2:00.

A: Oh, that's OK. I understand.

B: Maybe you could get Jack to take you.

A: Good idea.

2:06
🔊 **Ways to indicate acceptance**
I understand.
No problem.
Don't worry about it.

B 🔊 2:05 **Rhythm and intonation** Listen again and repeat. Then practice the Conversation Model with a partner.

NOW YOU CAN   Get someone else to do something

I wonder if you could do me a favor . . .

A Review the Vocabulary. On a separate sheet of paper, write a list of three requests for a favor.

B **Pair work** Change the Conversation Model to create a new conversation. Use one of the favors from your list. Your partner gives a reason for turning down your request and suggests getting someone else to do it. Then change roles.

A: ...., I wonder if you could do me a favor.

B: .... What do you need?

A: .... Do you think you could ....?

B: I would, but ....

A: Oh, that's OK. ....

B: Maybe you could get ....

A: ....

Reasons to turn down a request
- I'm running late for an appointment.
- I have a meeting in an hour.
- I'm expecting an important phone call.
- Your own reason: —

Don't stop! Make other suggestions.
What about ___ ?
Why don't you ask ___ ?

C **Change partners** Try to get someone else to do you a favor.

GOAL **Request express service**

VOCABULARY *Services*

A 🔊 2:07 Read and listen. Then listen again and repeat.

1 dry-clean a suit

2 repair shoes

3 frame a picture

4 deliver a package

5 lengthen / shorten a skirt

6 print a sign

7 copy a report

B **Pair work** Name other things you can get these services for.

> 66 You can also dry-clean sweaters or pants. 99

GRAMMAR *The passive causative*

Use a form of <u>have</u> or <u>get</u> with an object and a past participle to talk about arranging services. There is no difference in meaning between <u>have</u> and <u>get</u>.

	object	past participle
I **had**	my suits	**dry-cleaned**.
They**'re having**	the office	**painted** tomorrow.
She **can get**	her sandals	**repaired** in an hour.

Remember: In the passive voice, a <u>by</u> phrase is used when the information is important.

We had the office painted last week. It looks great. (no <u>by</u> phrase)
We're having the office painted **by Royal Painting Services**. They're the best!

GRAMMAR BOOSTER ▸ p. 126
• *The passive causative: the <u>by</u> phrase*

A **Grammar practice** Write questions using the passive causative. Write three questions with <u>have</u> and three with <u>get</u>.

1 Would it be possible to / these pictures / frame?
....

2 Could I / these sandals / repair / here?
....

3 Where can I / this bowl / gift wrap?
....

4 Can I / these shirts / dry-clean / by tomorrow?
....

5 Is it possible to / my hair / cut / at 3:00 / by George?
....

6 Would you / these photos / print / before 6:00?
....

B 🔊 **Listening comprehension** Listen to the conversations. Complete each statement with the item and the service. Use passive causatives.

1 She needs to get her ....
2 He wants to get his ....
3 She's thinking about having a ....
4 He needs to have his ....

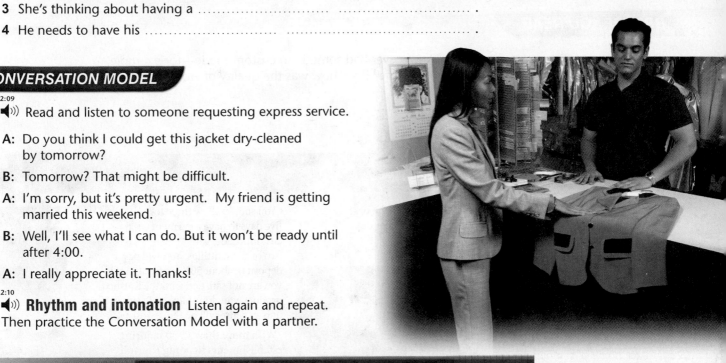

CONVERSATION MODEL

A 🔊 Read and listen to someone requesting express service.

A: Do you think I could get this jacket dry-cleaned by tomorrow?

B: Tomorrow? That might be difficult.

A: I'm sorry, but it's pretty urgent. My friend is getting married this weekend.

B: Well, I'll see what I can do. But it won't be ready until after 4:00.

A: I really appreciate it. Thanks!

B 🔊 **Rhythm and intonation** Listen again and repeat. Then practice the Conversation Model with a partner.

NOW YOU CAN   Request express service

A **Pair work** Change the Conversation Model. Use the ideas to request an express service and give a reason for why it's urgent. Then change roles.

A: Do you think I could .... by ....?

B: ....? That might be difficult.

A: I'm sorry, but it's pretty urgent. ....

B: Well, I'll see what I can do. But it won't be ready until ....

A: ....!

Ideas for express services
- frame a [photo / painting / drawing / diploma]
- dry-clean a [suit / dress / sweater]
- lengthen or shorten a [dress / skirt / pants]

Ideas for why it's urgent
- Someone is coming to visit.
- You're going on [a vacation / a business trip].
- There's going to be [a party / a meeting].
- Your own idea: ___

Don't stop!
- Say you need to have the service completed earlier.
- Ask how much it will cost.

 Be sure to recycle this language.

I owe you one!	I know this is last minute.
Thanks a million.	I won't keep you any longer.
You're a lifesaver!	

B **Change partners** Request other express services.

31

BEFORE YOU READ

Warm-up Have you or someone you know ever had something custom-made—for example, something to wear or something for your home? If so, how was the quality of workmanship?

READING 2:11

The Tailors of Hong Kong

The famous Hong Kong 24-hour suit is a thing of the past, but tailors there are still reliable: You can trust them if they say they'll have your clothes custom-made in just a few days.

Today, prices are quite reasonable—not as low as they used to be, but they're often about what you'd pay for a ready-made garment back home. The difference, of course, is that a tailor-made garment should fit you perfectly. Most tailors are extremely professional. The workmanship and quality of the better established shops rival even those of London's Savile Row—but at less than half the price!

Tailors in Hong Kong are very helpful and are willing to make almost any garment you want. Most offer a wide range of fabrics from which to choose, from cotton and linen to very fine wools, cashmere, and silk.

At your first fitting, the tailor will take your measurements.

You should allow three to five days to have a garment custom-made, with at least two or three fittings. You will pay a deposit of about 50% up front. But if you are not satisfied with the finished product, you don't have to accept it. Your only expense will be the deposit.

With more than 2,500 tailoring establishments in Hong Kong, it shouldn't be any problem finding one. Some of the most famous are located in hotel arcades and shopping complexes, but the more upscale the location, the higher the prices.

Once you've had something custom-made and your tailor has your measurements, you will more than likely be able to order additional clothing online, even after you've returned home!

You can choose from a variety of fabrics.

Tailors will make almost any garment you want—suits, evening gowns, wedding dresses, leather jackets, and shirts.

Source: Information from *Frommer's Hong Kong*

A Identify supporting details Check the statements that are true, according to the article. Find information in the Reading to support your answers.

1 ☐ You used to be able to get a suit made in one day in Hong Kong.

2 ☐ Having a suit custom-made in Hong Kong is always less expensive than buying one at home.

3 ☐ If you buy a garment on Savile Row in London, you will pay about twice as much as you would pay for one custom-made in Hong Kong.

4 ☐ If you are not satisfied with the finished garment, you can refuse to accept it and pay only 50% of the total cost.

5 ☐ If you want to pay a lower price for a custom-made garment, go to an upscale hotel shopping arcade.

B Activate language from a text Find these adjectives in the Reading on page 32. Complete the descriptions, using the adjectives.

reliable   reasonable   helpful   professional

1 I find Portello's to be really .... compared to other places. I've shopped around and I can't find another service with such low prices.

2 What I like about Link Copy Services is that they're so .... Even if the job is a bit unusual, they're willing to try.

3 Jamco Design is extremely .... You never have to worry about their doing anything less than an excellent job.

4 Dom's Auto Repair is incredibly .... If they promise to have a job ready in an hour, you can be sure that they will.

On your *ActiveBook* Self-Study Disc:
Extra Reading Comprehension Questions

PRONUNCIATION   *Emphatic stress to express enthusiasm*

2:12

🔊 Read and listen. Then listen again and repeat. Finally, read each statement on your own, using emphatic stress.

1 They're **REAL**ly reliable.

2 They're in**CRED**ibly helpful.

3 They're ex**TREME**ly professional.

4 They're **SO** reasonable.

NOW YOU CAN   Evaluate the quality of service

A Frame your ideas Complete the chart with services you or someone you know uses. Write the name of the business and list the reasons why you use that business. Then compare charts with a partner.

Reasons for choosing a business
• speed
• reliability
• price
• workmanship
• location
• efficiency
• professionalism
• other: ___

Service	Name of business	Reason
laundry / dry cleaning		
repairs		
tailoring		
delivery		
haircuts		
copying		
other: _____		

B Discussion Recommend local businesses from your chart. Explain why you or other people use them. Use the active and passive causatives.

❝I always get my clothes dry-cleaned at Quick Clean. They're near my home and their prices are reasonable.❞

❝I rarely have my shoes repaired. But I hear that Al's Shoes is fast and reliable.❞

33

GOAL **Plan a meeting or social event**

A 2:13 ◀))) **Vocabulary** • *Planning an event* Read and listen. Then listen again and repeat.

make a list of attendees

pick a date, time, and place

make a budget

assign responsibilities

plan an agenda

send out an announcement

arrange catering

set up the room

B **Pair work** Have you ever taken any of these steps to plan an event, such as a meeting or party? Which of the activities do you think you would be the best at doing? Use the Vocabulary.

A 2:14 ◀))) **Listen for main ideas** Listen to the conversation and answer the questions.

1 What kind of event are they planning?
....

2 How many people will come to the event?
....

3 Is it a formal or informal event?
....

4 Which of the following are mentioned as part of the event? (music / food / a lecture / dancing / meetings)
....

B 2:15 ◀))) **Listen for order of details** Listen again and number the activities in the order they will occur. Circle the activities she'll do herself.

	make a list of attendees
1	pick a date and time
	pick a location
	make a budget
	assign responsibilities
	send out announcements
	arrange catering
	arrange music
	set up the room

A Frame your ideas Take the survey. Compare answers with a partner.

Check which event activities you would rather do. Choose from Column A or B.

What type of person are YOU?

Column A	Column B
○ make a budget	○ spend money
○ assign responsibilities	○ take responsibility
○ plan an agenda	○ be a presenter
○ arrange catering	○ cook food
○ get people to set up the room	○ set up the room
○ leave before cleanup	○ stick around to clean up

If you chose four or more from Column A, you're a **BORN ORGANIZER!**

If you chose four or more from Column B, you're a **TEAM PLAYER!**

B Notepadding In a group, plan a meeting or social event for your class. Choose the type of event and discuss what needs to be done. Write the activities and assign responsibilities. Discuss dates, times, and locations.

Type of event:	Location:
Date and time:	
Activity	**Name**

Some ideas

- A special meeting
- An English practice day

An end-of-year ⎫
New Year's Eve ⎬ party
A TGIF* ⎭
*Thank goodness it's Friday!

A talent ⎫ show
A *Top Notch Pop* karaoke ⎭

♻ **Be sure to recycle this language.**

Why don't we ___?	What needs to be done [first]?
Why don't you ___?	That's a [good idea. / great idea. /
How about ___?	good point.]
What about ___?	That would be great.
I think ___.	That sounds ___.

C Discussion Present your plans to your class. Then choose the best plan.

Review

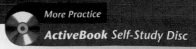

More Practice

ActiveBook *Self-Study Disc*

grammar · vocabulary · listening
reading · speaking · pronunciation

A ◀)) **Listening comprehension** Listen to each conversation.
Write a sentence to describe what the customer needs and when.
Listen again if necessary.

Example: He'd like to get his shoes shined by tomorrow morning.

1 ....

2 ....

3 ....

4 ....

B Complete each question or request with any noun that makes sense with
the passive causative verb.

1 Can I get my .... dry-cleaned by tomorrow?

2 I'd like to have this .... lengthened.

3 Where can I get this .... shortened?

4 Can you tell me where I can get some .... copied?

5 Where did she get her .... framed?

6 How much did he pay to have his .... repaired?

7 What's the best place to get some .... printed?

8 Where can I go to get my .... delivered quickly?

> 2:17/2:18
> ♪ **Top Notch Pop**
> "I'll Get Back to You"
> Lyrics p. 149

C Complete each causative statement in your own way. Remember
to use either the base form or the infinitive form of a verb.

1 At the end of the meal, she had the waiter ....

2 We got the travel agent ....

3 When I was young, my mother always made me ....

4 When you arrive, you should get the hotel ....

5 Don't forget to have the gas station attendant ....

6 I can never get my friends ....

D **Writing** Do you think being a procrastinator is a serious problem?
On a separate sheet of paper, explain your views by giving examples
from personal experience.

Some possible examples
- getting things repaired
- having things cleaned
- paying bills
- making plans for a vacation
- keeping in touch with people

> **WRITING BOOSTER** ▸ p. 142
> - *Supporting an opinion with
>   personal examples*
> - *Guidance for Exercise D*

Paul's Difficult Day

Game Study the pictures for one minute, paying attention to the time in each picture. Then close your books. Ask and answer questions about the photos, using the causative. Start like this:

What does Paul need to get done at 2:00?

Pair work Create a conversation for each situation. Start like this:

Do you think I could get this ___ by ___?

Story Close your books. In a small group, tell the story of Paul's day. Start like this:

At 9:00, Paul needed to get ___ . . .

NOW I CAN...

- [ ] Get someone else to do something.
- [ ] Request express service.
- [ ] Evaluate the quality of service.
- [ ] Plan a meeting or social event.

Reading for Pleasure

search | help | feedback

Looking for a good classic? Check out our recommendations. Click on a category for more.

FICTION

Novels	Mysteries	Thrillers	Romance	Science fiction	Short stories

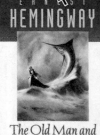  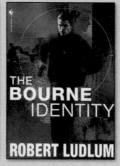   

Hemingway's exquisite novel. Read and reread by millions!

Who killed Charles McCarthy at the pool? And why? Detective Sherlock Holmes tries to solve another case.

A contemporary thriller that will have you on the edge of your seat!

No one does romance like Danielle Steele.

A strange object is found on the Moon. But who put it there? Arthur Clarke's masterpiece!

Beautiful short stories by the world's greatest and most beloved writers.

NON-FICTION

Biographies	Autobiographies	Travel	Memoirs	Self-help

  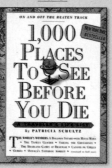  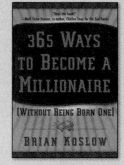

The true story of the amazing woman who inspired millions.

In Helen Keller's own words—her unforgettable story.

A must-read for real travelers—or even those who just dream about traveling!

The true story of writer Frank McCourt's surprising and funny experiences as a teacher in New York City.

Want to get rich? Brian Koslow shows you how.

A ◀))) 2:19 **Vocabulary** • *Types of books* Read and listen. Then listen again and repeat.

fiction		non-fiction	
a novel	a romance novel	a biography	a memoir
a mystery	science fiction	an autobiography	a self-help book
a thriller	short stories	a travel book	

B **Discussion** Do you prefer fiction or non-fiction? Have you ever read a book in English? How about a magazine or a newspaper? If not, what would you like to read? Why?

C 🔊 **Photo story** Read and listen to a conversation between two friends at a bookstore.

Lynn: Hey, Sophie! I've never run into you here before!

Sophie: Lynn! Good to see you. Looking for anything special?

Lynn: No, I'm just browsing. How about you?

Sophie: I'm just picking up some gardening magazines for my mom. She can't get enough of them . . . So, anything interesting?

Lynn: This one doesn't look bad. It's a biography of Helen Keller. What about you? Are you reading anything good these days?

Sophie: Well, I've got a new mystery on my night table, but I can't seem to get into it. I guess mysteries just aren't my thing.

Lynn: I know what you mean. They put me to sleep.

Sophie: Well, you're a big reader. I wonder if you could recommend something for me.

Lynn: Have you read the new John Grisham thriller?

Sophie: No, I haven't. I didn't know he had a new book out.

Lynn: Well, I can't put it down. It's a real page-turner.

Sophie: Thanks for the tip! Do you think I could borrow it when you're done with it?

Lynn: Of course. If you can wait till the end of the week, I'd be happy to lend it to you.

D **Think and explain** Classify each of the six underlined expressions from the Photo Story by its meaning. Explain your choices.

Likes	Doesn't like

E **Paraphrase** Say each of the underlined verbs and phrasal verbs in your own way.

1 I've never <u>run into</u> you here before.

2 I'm just <u>browsing</u>.

3 I'm <u>picking up</u> some gardening magazines for my mom.

4 Do you think I could <u>borrow</u> it when you're finished?

5 I'd be happy to <u>lend</u> it to you.

F **Group work** What percentage of your total reading time do you spend on the following reading materials? (Make sure it adds up to 100%!) Compare percentages with your classmates.

magazines		fiction	
newspapers		non-fiction	
the Internet		other	

GOAL   **Recommend a book**

VOCABULARY   *Ways to describe a book*

A 🔊 2:21 Read and listen. Then listen again and repeat.

It's **a page-turner.** *It's so interesting that you want to keep reading it.*

It's **a cliff-hanger.** *It's so exciting that you can't wait to find out what happens next.*

It's **a best-seller.** *It's very popular and everyone is buying copies.*

It's **a fast read.** *It's easy and enjoyable to read.*

It's **hard to follow.** *It's difficult to understand.*

It's **trash.** *It's very poor quality.*

B Pair work Discuss which types of books you find the most interesting. Use the Vocabulary from here and page 38.

> 66 I prefer thrillers. A thriller is usually a pretty fast read. It helps pass the time. 99

GRAMMAR   *Noun clauses*

A noun clause is a group of words that functions as a noun. A noun clause can be introduced by <u>that</u> and often functions as the direct object of a "mental activity" verb.

> I didn't know **that he wrote that book.**
> I think **that Junot Diaz's novels are fantastic.**
> She forgot **that Andrew Morton wrote biographies.**

When a noun clause functions as a direct object, <u>that</u> may be omitted.

> I didn't know **he wrote that book.**

In short answers, use <u>so</u> to replace a noun clause after the verbs <u>think</u>, <u>believe</u>, <u>guess</u>, and <u>hope</u>.

> A: Does Steven King have a new book out?
> B: I think **so.** / I believe **so.** / I guess **so.** / I hope **so.**
> (so = that Steven King has a new book out)

Other clauses with <u>that</u> often follow certain predicate adjectives. The word <u>that</u> can be omitted.

> We're both **disappointed** (that) his new book isn't very good.
> Were you **surprised** (that) the ending was sad?

Noun clauses and other clauses with <u>that</u> often follow these verbs and adjectives.

Verbs		Adjectives
agree	hear	disappointed
think	see	happy
believe	understand	sad
feel	hope	sorry
suppose	forget	sure
doubt	remember	surprised
guess	know	

Be careful!
I don't think **so.** / I don't believe **so.**
BUT I guess **not.** / I hope **not.**
NOT ~~I don't guess so.~~ / ~~I don't hope so.~~

GRAMMAR BOOSTER ▸ p. 126

• *More verbs and adjectives that can be followed by clauses with <u>that</u>*

Grammar practice On a separate sheet of paper, respond to each question with a clause using <u>that</u>. Use the prompts.

What has the author Monica Ali been up to lately? (write / a new novel)

> I think that she has written a new novel.

1 Where does the story take place? (in London / I guess)

2 What does Amy Tan usually write about? (mother-daughter relationships / I believe)

3 Where does Mario Vargas Llosa's novel *The Feast of the Goat* take place? (in the Dominican Republic / I hear)

4 What kind of book is Dan Brown going to write next? (another thriller / I hope)

Sentence stress in short answers with _so_

A 🔊 2:22 Read and listen. Notice the stress on the verb in short answers with <u>so</u>. Then listen again and repeat.

1 Are there a lot of characters in the story?   I **THINK** so.

2 Has she read that book yet?   I don't **THINK** so.

3 Do you think this thriller will be good?   I **HOPE** so.

4 Does the story have a happy ending?   I be**LIEVE** so.

B **Pair work** Ask and answer <u>yes</u> / <u>no</u> questions about your future plans. Respond with short answers, using <u>think</u>, <u>believe</u>, <u>hope</u>, or <u>guess</u>.

❝ Are you going to read anything this weekend? ❞   ❝ I think so. ❞

CONVERSATION MODEL

A 🔊 2:23 Read and listen to someone recommend a book.

A: Have you been reading anything interesting lately?

B: Actually, I'm reading a thriller called _Don't Close Your Eyes_.

A: I've never heard of that one. Is it any good?

B: Oh, I think it's great. It's a cliff-hanger. How about you?

A: I've just finished a Hemingway novel, _The Old Man and the Sea_. I highly recommend it.

B 🔊 2:24 **Rhythm and intonation** Listen again and repeat. Then practice the Conversation Model with a partner.

NOW YOU CAN   Recommend a book

A **Notepadding** Write some notes about a book you've read, or choose one of the books here.

Type of book:
Title:
Author:
What is it about?
Your recommendation:

B **Pair work** Change the Conversation Model, using the Vocabulary and your notepad.

A: Have you been reading anything interesting lately?

B: Actually, ...

A: .... heard of that one. Is it any good?

B: Oh, I think .... It's .... How about you?

A: ....

> **Don't stop!**
> Ask questions about the book.
> What's it about?
> Where does it take place?
> Why did you decide to read it?

FICTION

The Interpreter
by Charles Randolph

Silvia Broome is an interpreter at the United Nations who hears a secret plan to kill a state leader. But is she telling the truth?

The Time Machine
by H. G. Wells

A man builds a time machine and goes into the future, where he finds that people have become fearful, child-like creatures. But what are they afraid of?

NON-FICTION

New York
by Vicki Stripton

Every year, millions of tourists visit "the city that never sleeps." Read about its history, its sights, and its people.

Martin Luther King
by Coleen Degnan-Veness

In the U.S. in the 1950s and 60s, blacks did not have equal rights. But Martin Luther King had a dream —blacks and whites living together happily. He led peaceful protests and changed the country—and the world.

GOAL | **Offer to lend something**

CONVERSATION MODEL

A 🔊 2:25 Read and listen to someone offering to lend a magazine.

A: Is that the latest issue of *Car Magazine*?

B: Yes, it is.

A: Could you tell me where you bought it? I can't find it anywhere.

B: At the newsstand across the street. But I think it's sold out.

A: Too bad. There's an article in there I'm dying to read.

B: You know, I'd be happy to lend it to you when I'm done with it.

A: Really? That would be great. Thanks!

B 🔊 2:26 **Rhythm and intonation** Listen again and repeat. Then practice the Conversation Model with a partner.

GRAMMAR | *Noun clauses: embedded questions*

GRAMMAR BOOSTER ▶ p. 127

- Embedded questions:
  - usage and common errors
  - punctuation
  - with infinitives
- Noun clauses as subjects and objects

Noun clauses sometimes include embedded questions. Use **if** or **whether** to begin embedded **yes** / **no** questions. (**If** and **whether** have the same meaning.)

Yes / no questions	**Embedded yes / no questions**
Is that magazine any good?	Tell me **if that magazine is any good.**
Did he like the article?	I'd like to know **whether he liked the article.**
Have you finished that newspaper?	Could you tell me **if you've finished that newspaper?**
Can I borrow your brochure?	I wonder **whether I could borrow your brochure.**

Use a question word to begin embedded information questions.

Information questions	**Embedded information questions**
What's the article about?	Tell me **what the article's about.**
Why did you decide to read it?	Could you tell me **why you decided to read it?**
Who's the writer?	I wonder **who the writer is.**
Who recommended the article?	Do you know **who recommended the article?**
Who(m) is it written for?	Can you tell me **who(m) it's written for?**
Whose magazine is it?	I'd like to know **whose magazine it is.**
When was it written?	Would you tell me **when it was written?**
Where is the writer from?	Do you know **where the writer is from?**

Be careful!
Use normal word order (not question word order) in embedded questions.
Don't say:
I wonder ~~who is~~ the writer.
Do you know ~~where is~~ the writer from?

A Find the grammar Underline three examples of noun clauses in the Photo Story on page 39. Which two are embedded questions?

B Grammar practice Change the questions to embedded questions.

1 Does she like to read?
I wonder ....

2 Where did you get that magazine?
Can you tell me .... ?

3 Is he a John Grisham fan?
I've been wondering ....

4 Why don't you read newspapers?
I'm curious ....

5 Who told you about the article?
I was wondering ....

6 When did you hear about the new website?
I'd like to know ....

C Pair work Complete the survey below. Then look at your partner's responses. Use embedded questions to learn more about your partner.

> " Tell me why you like to read photography magazines. "

> " I wonder what sections of the newspaper you like to read. "

What kinds of materials do you like to read?

MAGAZINES

- ○ World news
- ○ Sports
- ○ Photography
- ○ Computers and electronics
- ○ Entertainment
- ○ Music

- ○ Fashion
- ○ Economics
- ○ Health and fitness
- ○ Business
- ○ Food and cooking
- ○ Other _____

NEWSPAPER SECTIONS

- ○ World news
- ○ Local news
- ○ Sports
- ○ Business

- ○ Entertainment
- ○ Travel
- ○ Other _____

NOW YOU CAN   Offer to lend something

A Pair work Change the Conversation Model. Create a conversation in which you offer to lend your partner something that you are reading. Then change roles.

Don't stop!
Use more embedded questions.
  Could you tell me ___?
  Do you know ___?
  I wonder ___.

A: Is that .... ?

B: Yes, ...

A: Could you tell me where you bought it? I can't find it anywhere.

B: .... But I think it's sold out.

A: Too bad. ....

B: You know, I'd be happy to lend it to you when I'm done with it.

A: .... !

B Change partners Discuss and offer to lend another magazine, newspaper, or book.

GOAL | Describe your reading habits

BEFORE YOU LISTEN

A 2:27 🔊 **Vocabulary • *Some ways to enjoy reading*** Read and listen. Then listen again and repeat.

curl up with [a book]

read aloud [to someone]

listen to audio books

do puzzles

read [articles] online

skim through [a newspaper]

read electronic books / e-books

B Pair work Discuss which activities from the Vocabulary match the situations below. Explain your reasons.

- Is convenient for when you are driving
- Helps pass the time during a bus or train commute
- Is a good way to relax
- Is a way to keep up with the news

LISTENING COMPREHENSION

2:28
🔊 **Listen to take notes** Listen and take notes to answer these questions about each speaker. Listen again if necessary.

1 What kinds of reading material does he or she like?

2 When does he or she like to read?

3 Where does he or she like to read?

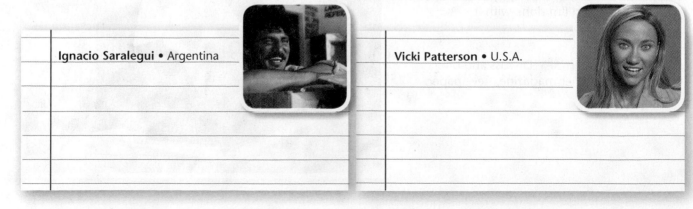

Su Yomei • Taiwan

Ignacio Saralegui • Argentina

Vicki Patterson • U.S.A.

A **Frame your ideas** Complete the questionnaire.

What are your reading habits?

1 Do you consider yourself to be a big reader? Why or why not?
_____
_____

2 Do you have any favorite authors? Who are they?
_____
_____

3 Do you prefer any particular types of books? Which types?
_____
_____

4 Are you a big newspaper reader? What sections of the paper do you prefer to read?
_____
_____

5 Do you read a lot of magazines? What kind?
_____
_____

6 Do you spend a lot of time reading online? Why or why not?
_____
_____

7 Have you ever read aloud to someone? Has anyone ever read aloud to you? When?
_____
_____

8 Do you listen to audio books? If so, do you like them?
_____
_____

9 When and where do you prefer to read the most?
_____
_____

10 Is there anything else you can add about your reading habits?
_____
_____

B **Pair work** Use the survey to interview your partner about his or her reading habits. Take notes on a separate sheet of paper.

C **Group work** Now tell your classmates about your partner's reading habits.

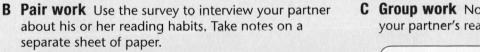
❝Ellen prefers to read in bed before she goes to sleep . . .❞

  Be sure to recycle this language.

I'd like to know . . .   I guess (that) . . .
Could you tell me . . . ?   I think (that) . . .
                              I suppose (that) . . .

45

GOAL **Discuss the quality of reading materials**

BEFORE YOU READ

Warm-up Do you—or does anyone you know—read comics? Do you think there's any value in reading them?

READING 2:29

Comics: trash or treasure?

In Japan, they're known as *manga*; in Latin America, *historietas* or *historias em quadrinhos*; in Italy, *fumetti*. Some people call them "graphic novels." But no matter what you call them, comics are a favorite source of reading pleasure for millions in many parts of the world.

In case you're wondering how popular they are, the best-selling comic in the U. S. sells about 4.5 million copies a year. Mexico's comic titles sell over 7 million copies a week. But Japan is by far the leading publisher of comics in the world. *Manga* account for nearly 40 percent of all the books and magazines published in Japan each year.

Ever since comics first appeared, there have been people who have criticized them. In the 1940s and 50s, many people believed that comics were immoral and that they caused bad behavior among young people. Even today, many question whether young people should read them at all.

They argue that reading comics encourages bad reading habits. In more recent years some comics have been criticized for including violence and sexual content.

On the other hand, some educators see comics as a way to get teenagers to choose reading instead of television and video games. And because of the art, a number of educators have argued that comics are a great way to get children to think creatively. Some recent research has suggested that the combination of visuals and text in comics may be one reason young people handle computers and related software so easily.

In many places, comics have been a convenient way to communicate social or political information. For example, in the 1990s, comics were used by the Brazilian health ministry to communicate information about AIDS. In Japan, the Education Ministry calls comics "a part of Japan's national culture, recognized and highly regarded abroad." Comics are increasingly being used for educational purposes, and many publishers there see them as a useful way of teaching history and other subjects.

No matter how you view them, comics remain a guilty pleasure for millions worldwide.

Sources: Associated Press, Ananova News Service, PRNewswire

In Japan, train station newsstands do a booming business selling *manga* during rush hour. And for true addicts, automatic vending machines that sell *manga* are everywhere.

Spider-Man® is one of the world's most recognizable and celebrated comic superheroes. Fifteen million Spider-Man comics are sold each year in 75 countries and in 22 languages.

A Recognize points of view List some reasons people criticize comics and defend them, according to the article.

Some reasons people criticize comics	Some reasons people defend comics

B Critical thinking Discuss the following questions.

1 What point of view do you think the writer of the article has about comics? Explain your reasons.

2 Why do you think comics are so popular around the world? Why do you think Japanese *manga* are so popular outside of Japan?

3 Why do you think some people find reading comics "a guilty pleasure"?

On your *ActiveBook* Self-Study Disc:
Extra Reading Comprehension Questions

NOW YOU CAN | Discuss the quality of reading materials

A Frame your ideas Complete the chart to explain your opinions about certain reading materials.

Types of materials	Who reads them?	Are they trash?		Your reasons
comics	boys, 12 to 17 years old	(Y)	N	I think they're violent and sexist.

Types of materials	Who reads them?	Are they trash?		Your reasons
comics		Y	N	
teen magazines		Y	N	
fashion magazines		Y	N	
sports magazines		Y	N	
movie magazines		Y	N	
romance novels		Y	N	
thrillers		Y	N	
horror magazines		Y	N	
sci-fi magazines		Y	N	
online blogs		Y	N	
newspapers		Y	N	
other:		Y	N	

B Pair work Compare the comments you wrote on your charts. Discuss your ideas. Then choose one type of reading material you both agree is trash and one you both agree is not. Prepare to explain your reasons to the class.

C Group work With a partner, compare the quality of two types of reading materlals. Explain your reasons to your classmates.

Text-mining (optional).
Underline language in the Reading on page 46 to use in the Group Work.
For example: "Many people question whether ..."

♻ **Be sure to recycle this language.**

Express an opinion
I think (that) . . .
I believe (that) . . .
I guess (that) . . .
In my opinion, . . .

Describe materials
I can't put ___ down.
I'm really into ___.
I can't get enough of ___.
They're a fast read.
I can't get into ___.
___ aren't my thing.
___ don't turn me on.
___ are hard to follow.

Review

More Practice
ActiveBook *Self-Study Disc*

grammar · vocabulary · listening
reading · speaking · pronunciation

A ◀)) **Listening comprehension** Listen to each conversation and write the
type of book each person is discussing. Then decide if the person likes the book.
Explain your answer.

Type of book	Likes it?	Explain your answer
1	Y N	
2	Y N	
3	Y N	
4	Y N	

B Write the name of each type of book.

1 A novel about people falling in love: ....

2 A book about a famous person: ....

3 A book that a famous person writes about his or her own life: ....

4 A very exciting novel with people in dangerous situations: ....

5 Books that are about factual information: ....

6 A strange fictional story about the future: ....

C Use the expressions in the box to change each question to an embedded
question. (Use each expression once.)

> I was wondering . . .   Could you tell me . . .   I don't know . . .
>
> I can't remember . . .   Would you please tell me . . .

1 Where does the story take place?

....

2 Who is the main character in the novel?

....

3 How much was that newspaper?

....

4 How do you say this in English?

....

5 What does this word mean?

....

2:31/2:32
♫ **Top Notch Pop**
"A True Life Story"
Lyrics p. 149

D **Writing** On a separate sheet of paper, write a review of something you've read—a book or
an article from a magazine, a newspaper, or the Internet.

* Summarize what it was about.

* Make a recommendation to the reader.

WRITING BOOSTER ▸ p. 143

* Summarizing
* Guidance for Exercise D

Pair work

1 Create a conversation for the man and woman in which he asks about the book she is reading. She makes a recommendation. He asks if he can borrow the book. Start like this:

Are you reading anything interesting?

2 Use the pictures to create a conversation in which the man and woman discuss their reading habits. For example:

I usually like to curl up in bed with a good book.

Game Close your books. Make an "I" statement about the reading habits of the man or woman.
Your partner guesses if it's the man or the woman.
For example:

A: I like to do the puzzles in the newspaper.
B: I think it's the __.

NOW I CAN...

- ☐ Recommend a book.
- ☐ Offer to lend something.
- ☐ Describe my reading habits.
- ☐ Discuss the quality of reading materials.

Natural Disasters

GOALS After Unit 5, you will be able to:

1 Convey a message.
2 Report news.
3 Describe natural disasters.
4 Prepare for an emergency.

YESTERDAY AS THE APEX OF THE FIGHT AGAINST INFLUENZA **WAS** Fogarty, is shown in an unusual posture. He is sitting down while Mrs. Genevieve Murray is making san. Mrs. E. P. Stimpson and Mrs. Leone Phelps, leaders of Red Cross work, assigning "mothers" to care ture. Mrs. Eugene H. Folsom (standing) and her Red Cross girls are caught in the picture to the right, in the midst of a busy day, making masks.

RED CROSS WORKERS SUCCEED IN MEETING HEAVY CALLS FOR AID IN BATTLE ON INFLUENZA

Women of Mother Kind Still Urgently Needed for Ser ... in Stricken Homes; Mask Profiteers Scored;

OPEN AIR AND VACCINE WILL FIGHT DISEASE

300,000 Cases in State Are Feared Unless Patients Kept in Uncovered Hospitals

The influenza epidemic of 1918–1919 left an estimated 25 million people dead worldwide.

World Week
US EDITION

SNOWBOUND
Record snowfall paralyzes Washington D.C.

In February 2010, two major blizzards dumped historic levels of snow on the Washington D.C. area, causing travel delays, school closures, and power outages.

WORLD NEWS *Famine in Ethiopia*

In 1984, hungry communities in Ethiopia faced one of the worst food crises in history.

A Discussion Discuss one or more of the following topics about the content of the news.

1 Do you think or worry about epidemics, famines, and weather emergencies? When stories about these events appear in the news, are you interested in reading about them?

2 Why do newspapers often put this information on the front page?

3 What percentage of the news is about disasters and emergencies?

4 Not all disasters are natural disasters (caused by nature). What are some other kinds of disasters? How are they caused?

B 🔊 **Photo story** Read and listen to a conversation about a natural disaster.

Rachel: Oh, my goodness. Take a look at this!

Tom: Why? What's going on?

Rachel: There's this enormous flood in Slovakia—look at these people on the roof! The water's up to the second floor. And look at these cars. I sure hope there was no one in them.

Tom: That sounds horrendous. Any word on casualties?

Rachel: It says, "No reports of deaths or injuries so far . . . ." But it's in the middle of a city, for goodness sake. The death toll could end up being huge.

Tom: And can you imagine the property damage?

Rachel: Well, they estimate almost 50% of the houses in town are under water already.

Tom: What a disaster!

Rachel: I wonder how this flood compares to the one they had in New Orleans a few years back. Remember that?

Tom: You bet I do. How could anyone forget? And that flooded almost half the city too.

Rachel: Let's turn on CNN. They usually have breaking news about stuff like this.

C **Focus on language** Complete each statement with words or phrases from the Photo Story.

1 Two words that mean very big are .... and ....

2 The number of .... indicates the number of people who are injured or killed in an event.

3 A two-word phrase that means the destruction of or harm to buildings, cars, and other things that belong to victims of an event is ....

4 A two-word expression that is used to describe the first news reports of an important event that is happening at the present is ....

D **Pair work** Where do you get your news? Complete the chart with the news sources you and your partner use.

	My news sources	My partner's news sources
a newspaper		
a weekly news magazine		
TV newscasts		
radio news reports		
Internet news sites		
word of mouth		

E **Discussion** Which do you think are the best sources for breaking news? For weather forecasts? For emergency information? Explain your reasons. Give examples.

GOAL | **Convey a message**

GRAMMAR | *Indirect speech: imperatives*

To report what someone said without quoting the exact words, use indirect speech. Don't use quotation marks when you write indirect speech.
> Direct speech: Peter said, "**Be careful if you go out during the storm.**"
> Indirect speech: Peter said **to be careful if you go out during the storm.**

> *Indirect speech is a kind of noun clause. It is the direct object following a reporting verb such as <u>say</u>, <u>tell</u>, or <u>ask</u>.*

An imperative in direct speech becomes an infinitive in indirect speech.
> They said, "**Read** the weather report." → They said **to read** the weather report.
> She says, "**Don't go out** without a full tank of gas." → She says **not to go out** without a full tank of gas.

Change time expressions and pronouns in indirect speech as necessary.
> She told Dan, "Call **me tomorrow**." → She told Dan to call **her the next day**.

GRAMMAR BOOSTER ▸ p. 129
• *Direct speech: punctuation rules*

A Grammar practice On a separate sheet of paper, rewrite each statement in indirect speech, making necessary changes.

1 Martha told me, "Be home before the snowstorm."

> *Martha told me to be home before the snowstorm.*

2 Everyone is saying, "Get ready for a big storm."

3 The radio says, "Get supplies of food and water in case the roads are closed."

4 They told her, "Don't be home too late this afternoon."

5 Maria always tells him, "Don't leave your doors open."

B Pair work For each sentence, say what you think the speaker's original words were. Take turns.

1 He told them to call him when it starts raining.

> ❝ Please call me when it starts raining. ❞

2 The police said to leave a window or door open when there's going to be a severe storm.

3 She told his parents to read the emergency instructions in the newspaper.

4 Ray told Allison to look for the story about him in the paper the next day.

5 She asked him to pick up some supplies for her on the way home.

6 They told me not to wait until the snow gets heavy.

CONVERSATION MODEL

A 🔊 3:03 Read and listen to someone conveying a message.

A: I'm on the phone with your parents. Would you like to say hello?

B: I would, but I'm running late.

A: Anything you'd like me to tell them?

B: Yes. Please tell them to turn on the TV. There's a storm on the way.

A: Will do.

B 🔊 3:04 **Rhythm and intonation** Listen again and repeat. Then practice the Conversation Model with a partner.

3:05

A 🔊 Notice the rhythm of sentences in direct and indirect speech. Read and listen. Then listen again and repeat.

1 He said, [pause] "Be home before midnight." → He said to be home before midnight.

2 I told your parents, [pause] "Get a flu shot at the clinic." → I told your parents to get a flu shot at the clinic.

B **Pair work** Take turns reading aloud the sentences in the Grammar Practice on page 52. Read both the original sentences and the sentences you wrote, using correct rhythm for direct and indirect speech.

NOW YOU CAN **Convey a message**

A **Notepadding** Read the possible excuses and messages. Then write three more excuses and three more messages.

B **Pair work** Change the Conversation Model. Role-play conveying a message. Use any of the excuses / messages on the telephone display. Then change roles.

    A: I'm on the phone with .... Would you like to say hello?

    B: I would, but ....

    A: Anything you'd like me to tell ....?

    B: Yes. Please tell .... to ....

    A: ....

Don't stop!
Continue the conversation.
Ask your partner:
• what time he or she will be home.
• to do you a favor.
• to call you later.

C **Change partners** Practice the conversation again. Use another message. Use another excuse.

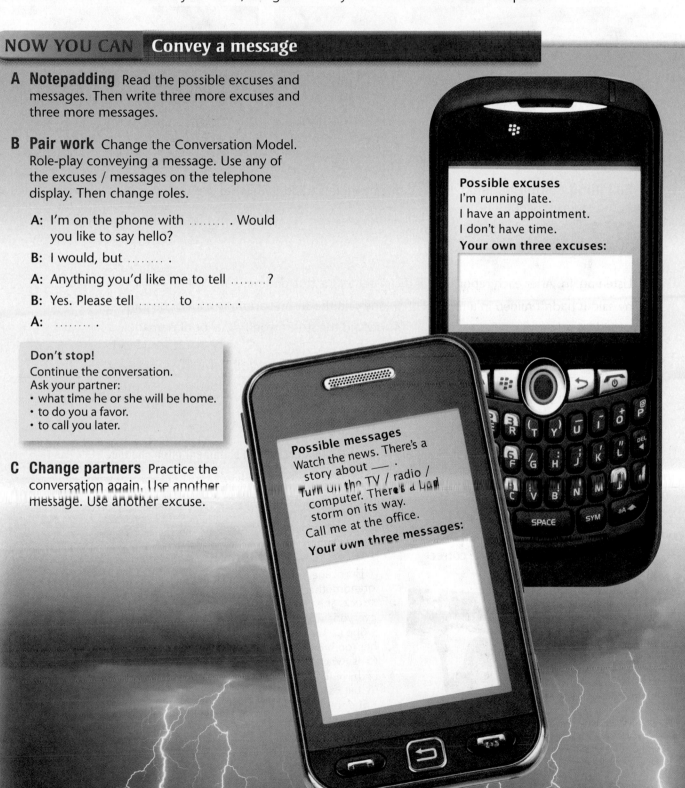

Possible excuses
I'm running late.
I have an appointment.
I don't have time.
Your own three excuses:

Possible messages
Watch the news. There's a story about —— .
Turn on the TV / radio / computer. There's a bad storm on its way.
Call me at the office.
Your own three messages:

GOAL   Report news

VOCABULARY   *Severe weather and other natural disasters*

A 🔊 **3:06** Read and listen. Then listen again and repeat.

a tornado

a hurricane / typhoon

a flood

a landslide

a drought

B 🔊 **3:07** **Listening comprehension** Listen to the news. Infer, and then write the kind of event the report describes.

1 ....   3 ....

2 ....   4 ....

C 🔊 **3:08** Listen again. After each report, say if the statement is true or false.

1 She said it hadn't rained in a month.   3 She said the storm had done a lot of damage.

2 He said it hadn't rained for a week.   4 He said the storm won't do a lot of damage.

GRAMMAR   *Indirect speech: say and tell—tense changes*

Use tell when you mention the listener. Use say when you don't.
Maggie **told her parents** to stay home. (listeners mentioned)
Maggie **said** to stay home. (listeners not mentioned)

When say and tell are in the past tense, the verbs in the indirect speech statement often change. Present becomes past. Past becomes past perfect.
They said, "The weather **is** awful." → They said (that) the weather **was** awful.
Dan said, "We all **had** the flu." → Dan **said** (that) they all **had had** the flu.

GRAMMAR BOOSTER ▸ p. 129
• *Indirect speech: optional tense changes*

A **Grammar practice** Circle the correct verbs for indirect speech.

My Great Grandmother Meets Hurricane Cleo

Hurricane Cleo struck the United States in August, 1964. My great grandmother, Ana, was traveling in Miami when the hurricane struck. She (1 said / told) me that she still remembers how scared everyone was.

She (2 said / told) me that the hotel (3 has called / had called) her room one morning and had (4 said / told) her that a big storm (5 is / was) on its way. They (6 said / told) that all hotel guests (7 have to / had to) stay in the hotel until the weather service (8 tell / said) that it (9 is / was) safe to leave.

She stayed in her room and she didn't know what happened until the storm was over. When she turned on the TV, the reports (10 said / told) that a lot of people (11 have been / had been) injured and that all the roads (12 are / were) flooded. She always (13 says / said) that she still (14 feels / felt) lucky to have survived Hurricane Cleo.

B Grammar practice Change each statement from direct speech to indirect speech, changing the verb tense in the indirect speech statement.

1 The TV reporter said, "The landslide is one of the worst in history."

> The TV reporter said the landslide was one of the worst in history.

2 He also said, "It caused the destruction of half the houses in the town."

3 My sister called and said, "There is no electricity because of the hurricane."

4 The newspaper said, "There was a tornado in the central part of the country."

5 The paper said, "The drought of 1999 was the worst natural disaster of the twentieth century."

6 After the great snowstorm in 1888, a New York newspaper reported, "The blizzard of '88 caused more damage than any previous storm."

CONVERSATION MODEL

A ◀)) 3:09 Read and listen to a conversation about the news.

A: What's going on in the news today?

B: Well, the *Times* says there was a terrible storm in the south.

A: Really?

B: Yes. It says lots of houses were destroyed.

A: What a shame.

B: But there haven't been any deaths.

A: Thank goodness for that.

B ◀)) 3:10 **Rhythm and intonation** Listen again and repeat. Then practice the Conversation Model with a partner.

NOW YOU CAN   Report news

A Notepadding Read each newspaper headline. Then write what it said on a separate sheet of paper, using indirect speech.

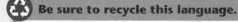

> The Morning Herald says there was an earthquake in Iran.

B Pair work Use the newspaper headlines to report what each newspaper says. Then change roles and newspaper headlines.

A: What's going on in the news today?

B: Well, ... says ....

A: Really?

B: Yes. It says ....

A: ....

Don't stop!
Discuss all the facts in the headlines. Express your reactions to the news.

♻ **Be sure to recycle this language.**

Oh, no!
What a disaster.
That's enormous / gigantic / huge / horrendous.

𝔐orning 𝔥erald
20,000 killed in earthquake in Iran

DAR POST
People flee flooded river valley

MERCURY
Avian influenza epidemic causes record deaths in Indonesia
Doctors urge children and elderly to receive vaccinations

National News
Drought causes severe famine
Thousands die of hunger

Village Times
Severe dust storm hits Kabul suburbs
Extreme damage to cars, buildings

C Change partners Practice the conversation again, using a different headline.

mild	!
moderate	!!
severe	!!!
deadly	!!!!
catastrophic	!!!!

A 3:11 **Vocabulary** • *Adjectives of severity*   Read and listen. Then listen again and repeat.

B Warm-up Have you or someone you know experienced a natural disaster? What kind of disaster was it? How severe was it? Tell the class about it.

READING 3:12

EARTHQUAKES

Earthquakes are among the deadliest natural disasters, causing the largest numbers of casualties, the highest death tolls, and the greatest destruction. In 1556 in China, the deadliest earthquake in history killed 830,000 people. But many other earthquakes have caused the deaths of more than 100,000 people, and it is not unusual, even in modern times, for an earthquake death toll to reach 20–30,000 people with hundreds of thousands left homeless and with countless injured. The floodwaters of the 2004 tsunami in Sumatra, which killed over 200,000 people, were caused by a catastrophic earthquake.

There are four factors that affect the casualty rate and economic impact of earthquakes: magnitude, location, quality of construction of buildings, and timing.

Magnitude

The magnitude, or strength, of an earthquake is measured on the Richter scale, ranging from 1 to 10, with 10 being the greatest. Earthquakes over 6 on the Richter scale are often deadly, and those over 8 are generally catastrophic, causing terrible damage.

Location

A severe earthquake that is located far from population centers does not cause the same damage as a less severe one that occurs in the middle of a city. As an example, in 1960, the strongest earthquake ever recorded, 9.5 magnitude on the Richter scale, struck in the Pacific Ocean near the Chilean coastline, destroying buildings, killing over 2,000, and injuring another 3,000 in regional cities near the coast. If this quake had struck a city directly, it would have been catastrophic, and hundreds of thousands might have been killed. Similarly, in Alaska, in 1964, a magnitude 9.2 quake hit an area with few people, and the death toll was 117.

Quality of Construction

Modern building construction techniques can lessen the death toll and economic impact of a moderate earthquake that would otherwise cause severe destruction of older-style buildings. In

Information source: underline:worldbookonline.com

The 2008 earthquake in Sichuan Province, China, was one of the deadliest earthquakes in recent history.

2010, a terrible earthquake in Port-au-Prince, the capital of Haiti, caused the destruction of a tremendous number of the city's buildings, mostly due to poor construction. In contrast, an even stronger earthquake later that year in Chile caused less destruction because of that country's use of earthquake-resistant construction.

Timing

Finally, the time of occurrence of an earthquake can affect the number of deaths and casualties. Earthquakes that occur in the night, when people are indoors, usually cause a greater death toll than ones that occur when people are outdoors.

Largest Earthquakes in the World Since 1950		
Place	**Year**	**Magnitude**
Off the coast of Chile	1960	9.5
Prince William Sound, Alaska, U.S.	1964	9.2
Off the west coast of northern Sumatra	2004	9.1
Kamchatka, Russia	1952	9.0
Chile	2010	8.8
Rat Islands, Alaska, U.S.	1965	8.7
Northern Sumatra, Indonesia	2005	8.6
Assam—Tibet	1950	8.6
Andreanof Islands, Alaska, U.S.	1957	8.6
Southern Sumatra, Indonesia	2007	8.5

A Paraphrase Rewrite the following statements in your own words, changing the underlined word or phrase.

1 The underline:magnitude of an earthquake is measured by the Richter scale.

2 There are four underline:factors that affect the destructive value of an earthquake.

3 Good construction techniques can underline:lessen the danger to people in buildings affected by an earthquake.

4 Damage is often underline:due to poor construction.

5 If an earthquake occurs near a major underline:population underline:center, more people will be affected.

B Confirm facts Answer the questions, according to the information in the article. Use indirect speech.

> 66 The article said the earthquake in 1556 was the deadliest in history. 99

1 Where did the deadliest earthquake in history take place?

2 Which earthquake had the highest recorded Richter scale reading?

On your *ActiveBook* Self-Study Disc:
Extra Reading Comprehension Questions

3 How can location affect the death toll of an earthquake?

4 What else can lessen the destruction and economic impact of an earthquake?

C Identify cause and effect Discuss how magnitude and timing affect the casualty rate and economic impact of earthquakes. Explain your ideas by putting together information from the article.

NOW YOU CAN   Describe natural disasters

A Pair work Partner A, read the fact sheet about the Jamaica hurricane. Partner B, read the fact sheet about the Philippines earthquake. In your own words, tell your partner about the disaster.

> 66 A hurricane hit Jamaica on September 20. There was a lot of property damage . . . 99

JAMAICA HURRICANE

Date:	September 20
Place:	Port Royal, Jamaica
Event:	hurricane

Property damage: many houses damaged by wind, flooding, and landslides

Casualties: hundreds homeless and missing

PHILIPPINES EARTHQUAKE

Date:	September 14
Place:	Manila, Philippines
Event:	earthquake, magnitude 6.7

Property damage: moderate in newer buildings, severe in older ones

Casualties: 200 deaths, many injuries, some severe and life-threatening

B Notepadding Choose one of the historic disasters from the list. Find information about it on the Internet, at a library, or in a bookstore. (Or choose a disaster you are already familiar with.) Write details about the disaster on your notepad.

Some historic disasters
- The San Francisco earthquake of 1906 (U.S.)
- The Bam earthquake of 2003 (Iran)
- The tsunami of 2004 (Indian Ocean)
- Hurricane Katrina 2005 (New Orleans, U.S.)
- The earthquake of 2010 (Haiti)
- A natural disaster of your choice: _____

Date:	
Place:	
Event:	
Property damage:	
Casualties:	

C Group work Make a news broadcast or presentation about the disaster you researched (or one of the disasters in A). Describe the natural disaster to your class.

♻ **Be sure to recycle this language.**

Type of disaster	Adjectives	Features
flood	mild	casualties
storm	moderate	injuries
landslide	severe	property damage
earthquake	deadly	death toll
flood	catastrophic	
famine		
epidemic		

Text-mining (optional)
Underline language in the Reading on page 56 to use in the Group Work.
For example:
" ―― was due to . . ."

GOAL **Prepare for an emergency**

BEFORE YOU LISTEN

A 🔊 **Vocabulary • Emergency preparations and supplies** Read and listen. Then listen again and repeat.

3:13

evacuate   to remove all people from an area that is too dangerous

an emergency   a very dangerous situation that requires immediate action

a power outage   an interruption in the flow of electrical power over a large area

a shelter   a safe place where people may go when the area they live in has been evacuated

a first-aid kit   a small box or package containing supplies to treat minor injuries and illnesses

a flashlight   a portable, battery-operated light

non-perishable food   food that doesn't need refrigeration, such as canned and dried food

> A battery-operated flashlight is a must when there is a power outage.

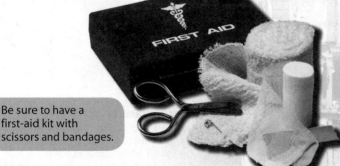

> Be sure to have a first-aid kit with scissors and bandages.

B Pair work With a partner, write sentences using the Vocabulary words and phrases.

> They tried to evacuate the entire population of the city before the flood, but lots of people refused to go.

LISTENING COMPREHENSION

A 🔊 **Listen for main ideas** Listen to an emergency radio broadcast. Write a sentence to describe the emergency the broadcaster is reporting.

3:14

....

....

B 🔊 **Listen for details** Listen again and correct each of the following false statements, using indirect speech.

3:15

Example: He said you should stand near windows during the storm.

> 🔊 No. He said not to stand near windows during the storm. 🔊

1 He said you should turn your refrigerator and freezer off.

2 He said that in case of a flood, you should put valuable papers on the lowest floor of your home.

3 He said you should read the newspapers for the location of shelters.

C Paraphrase What did the radio announcer say in the emergency radio broadcast? With a partner, discuss the questions and complete each statement in indirect speech. Listen again if necessary.

1 What should you do to get your car ready for an evacuation?

He said to ....

2 What should you do with outdoor furniture?

He said to ....

3 What should you buy for flashlights and portable radios?

He said to ....

4 What should you listen to in case of an evacuation?

He said to ....

5 How should you prepare to have food and water in case you have to stay indoors for several days?

He said to ....

NOW YOU CAN Prepare for an emergency

A Group work Choose an emergency from the list. Write plans for your emergency on the notepad. Provide a reason for each plan.

Plans	Reasons
Have 2 liters of water per person per day.	to have enough water in case the water is unsafe to drink

Type of emergency:	
Plans	Reasons

Kinds of emergencies
- a flood
- a tornado
- a severe storm (blizzard, hurricane, typhoon)
- an epidemic
- a famine
- a drought
- a landslide
- an earthquake

batteries

matches

bottled water

" Our group prepared for a storm. We said to be sure cell phones were working. A power outage might occur. "

B Present your plans to the class. Compare your plans.

Review

More Practice

ActiveBook *Self-Study Disc*

grammar · vocabulary · listening
reading · speaking · pronunciation

A 🔊 **Listening comprehension** Listen to the report. The reporter describes three kinds of disasters. Listen carefully and check the ones that fall into the categories she describes. Listen again if necessary.

3:16

		Disaster	Place	Year	Killed
☐	1	epidemic	worldwide	1917	20,000,000
☐	2	famine	Soviet Union	1932	5,000,000
☐	3	flood	China	1931	3,700,000
☐	4	drought	China	1928	3,000,000
☐	5	epidemic	worldwide	1914	3,000,000
☐	6	epidemic	Soviet Union	1917	2,500,000
☐	7	flood	China	1959	2,000,000
☐	8	epidemic	India	1920	2,000,000
☐	9	famine	Bangladesh	1943	1,900,000
☐	10	epidemic	China	1909	1,500,000

The 10 most deadly natural disasters of the 20th century

Source: CRED (Center for Research on the Epidemiology of Disasters)

3:17/3:18
🎵 **Top Notch Pop**
"Lucky to Be Alive"
Lyrics p. 149

B Complete each statement with the name of the disaster or emergency.

1 In ...., mud and soil cover the houses and can bury entire towns.

2 A widespread event in which many people become sick with the same illness is ....

3 A .... occurs when water from a river enters houses and roads.

4 A storm with high winds and rain is ....

5 When there is no rain for a long period of time, ... is said to occur.

6 In ...., there is not enough food and many people go hungry.

C Complete each indirect statement or question with <u>said</u> or <u>told</u>.

1 They .... me to call the office in the morning.

2 The students .... the test had been very difficult.

3 He .... the storm was awful.

4 Who .... us to get extra batteries?

D On a separate sheet of paper, rewrite the following indirect speech statements in direct speech.

1 She said they knew the reason there was so much property damage.

2 The radio announcer told the people to fill up their cars with gas before the storm.

3 I said not to tell the children about the storm.

4 He asked if the epidemic had been severe.

E On a separate sheet of paper, rewrite the following direct speech statements in indirect speech.

1 Robert told Marie, "Don't wait for the evacuation order."

2 Sylvia said, "I think the earthquake occurred during the night."

3 The emergency broadcast said, "Buy bottled water before the hurricane."

4 They told Marlene, "Call us the next day."

F Writing On a separate sheet of paper, write about how to prepare for an emergency. Choose an emergency and include information on what to do, what supplies to have, and what preparations to make.

WRITING BOOSTER ▸ p. 144

• *Organizing detail statements by order of importance*
• *Guidance for Exercise F*

TUESDAY

Tell a story Give the people names and relationships. Then tell the story of Tuesday and Wednesday in the pictures. For example:

On Tuesday, [Robert] called [his father] and told him to ___.

Pair work

1 Tell your partner what the TV announcer said on Tuesday. Then switch roles. Your partner tells you what the radio announcer said on Wednesday. Use indirect speech. For example:

The announcer said a tropical storm was coming...

2 Create a conversation between the two men on Tuesday. Start like this:

Hello, [Dad]. There's going to be a bad storm. They say ...

WEDNESDAY

NOW I CAN...

- Convey a message.
- Report news.
- Describe natural disasters.
- Prepare for an emergency.

61

Life Plans

GOALS | After Unit 6, you will be able to:

1 Explain a change in life and work plans.
2 Express regrets about past actions.
3 Discuss skills, abilities, and qualifications.
4 Discuss factors that promote success.

What's the best career for you?

Take this preference inventory to see which fields are the best match for you. Check all the activities you like to do.

- [ ] **work on experiments in a science laboratory**
- [ ] write songs
- [ ] **manage a department of a large business corporation**
- [ ] **repair furniture**
- [ ] **be a doctor and care for sick people**
- [ ] design the stage scenery for a play
- [ ] teach adults how to read
- [ ] **study a company's sales**
- [ ] **restore antique cars**
- [ ] **teach science to young people**
- [ ] take a creative writing class
- [ ] read to blind people
- [ ] **manage a company's sales representatives**
- [ ] make clothes to sell
- [ ] **interpret X-rays and other medical tests**
- [ ] make paintings and sculptures
- [ ] help couples with marriage problems
- [ ] **start my own business**
- [ ] **build houses**

Write the number of check marks you have by each color.

Field:
| | BUSINESS | | SCIENCE | | CRAFTS |
| | SOCIAL WORK | | ARTS |

A Discussion Talk about the following questions.

- Which field or fields did you have the most check marks in?
- Were you surprised by your results? Explain.
- What are some jobs or professions in that field?

B ◀)) **Photo story** Read and listen to a conversation about a career choice.

Charlotte: Dr. Miller, I wonder if I could pick your brain.

Dr. Miller: Sure, Charlotte. What's on your mind?

Charlotte: Well, I always thought I would go to engineering school, but now I'm not so sure anymore.

Dr. Miller: Well, it's not so unusual for a person your age to change her mind . . .

Dr. Miller: I must have changed mine ten times before I settled on medicine! Have you decided on something else?

Charlotte: Well, actually, I've developed an interest in the health field, and since you're a doctor . . .

Dr. Miller: Are you thinking of medicine?

Charlotte: Not specifically. Something related that doesn't take that long to study . . .

Charlotte: I know there are some good options, but I'm having trouble making up my mind.

Dr. Miller: Well, have you given any thought to becoming a physical therapist? It's a great field. You help people and there's always a job available.

Charlotte: Hmm. Physical therapy. I should have thought of that. I'll keep that in mind.

C **Focus on language** Look at the underlined expressions in the Photo Story. Then match each expression with its meaning.

...... **1** make up one's mind   **a** decide to do something else

...... **2** keep something in mind   **b** remember something

...... **3** be on one's mind   **c** think of something

...... **4** settle on   **d** decide to do something after considering conflicting choices

...... **5** change one's mind   **e** ask someone about something

...... **6** pick someone's brain   **f** make a final decision that won't change

D **Discussion** Is it common to change life or work plans before settling on something? Check any areas in which you have ever changed your mind. Then take a survey of the class. How many people have changed plans in each area? Discuss reasons people change their plans.

☐ a career or job choice

☐ a field of study

☐ a marriage

☐ a divorce

☐ the choice of a boyfriend or girlfriend

☐ other ....

GOAL | **Explain a change in life and work plans**

CONVERSATION MODEL

A 🔊 3:20 Read and listen to a conversation about a change in plans.

A: So what are you doing these days?

B: Well, I'm in dental school.

A: No kidding! I thought you had other plans.

B: That's right. I was going to be an artist, but I changed my mind.

A: How come?

B: Well, it's hard to make a living as a painter!

B 🔊 3:21 **Rhythm and intonation** Listen again and repeat. Then practice the Conversation Model with a partner.

GRAMMAR | *Future in the past: was / were going to and would*

Was / were going to is the past form of **be going to**. It is used to express or ask about future plans or expectations someone had in the past. It is often used for plans that changed or weren't achieved.

I **was going to get** married (but I didn't).   They **were going to study** art (but they didn't).
Was she **going to take** the course?   **Were** you **going to study** with Dr. Mellon?

Weren't you **going to study** law? (Yes, I was. / No, I wasn't.)
Where **were** they **going to work**? (In Kuala Lumpur.)
Who **was going to teach** this class? (My sister was.)

Would is the past form of **will**. It can also express future in the past. Use **would** + the base form in a noun clause direct object that describes future plans or expectations.

She thought she **would be** a doctor (but she changed her mind).
We always believed they **would get** married (but they never did).
They said they **would pay** for their daughter's studies (but they didn't).

Note: Noun clause direct objects can also use **was / were going to** + the base form.

They said they **were going to arrive** before noon (but they didn't).

> **Be careful!** Don't use **would** + a base form alone to express future plans or expectations. Use **was / were going to** instead.
>
> She was going to be a doctor.
> NOT She ~~would be~~ a doctor.

GRAMMAR BOOSTER ▸ p. 130

- *Expressing the future: review*
- *The future with will and be going to: review*

Grammar practice On a separate sheet of paper, write what each person said he or she was going to do. Write the sentences two ways, once with **was going to** and once with **said** and **would**.

❝I'm going to stop smoking.❞

❝I'm going to apply to law school.❞

❝I'm going to find a husband.❞

❝I'm going to marry Sylvia.❞

He was going to stop smoking. / He said he would stop smoking.

VOCABULARY   *Reasons for changing plans*

A 🔊 Read and listen. Then listen again and repeat.

I wanted to be a rock star, but **my tastes changed**.

I was going to be an artist, but **it's hard to make a living as an artist**.

I thought I would be a lawyer, but **I didn't pass the exam**.

I wanted to become a firefighter, but **my family talked me out of it**.

I was going to marry George, but **I just changed my mind**.

B Integrated practice On a separate sheet of paper, complete each sentence, using <u>would</u> where possible and a reason from the Vocabulary. Then compare reasons with a partner.

1 Laura thought / be / a doctor, but . . . .

2 I thought / become an astronaut, but . . . .

3 We were sure / Bill and Stella / get a divorce, but . . . .

4 Joe wanted / a writer but . . . .

C 🔊 **Listening comprehension** Listen to the conversations. Complete each statement about the decision each person made. Then listen again and use the Vocabulary to write the reason each person changed his or her mind.

1 She wanted to be a . . . . , but she changed her mind because . . . .

2 He was going to . . . . Jessica, but he didn't because . . . .

3 He always thought she would become a . . . . , but she didn't because . . . .

4 She was going to . . . . a Romanian named Andrei, but she didn't because . . . .

NOW YOU CAN   Explain a change in life and work plans

A Notepadding On the notepad, write some life, study, or work plans you had in the past, but which you changed your mind about. Write the reasons for the changes, using the Vocabulary or other reasons.

life plans:
study plans:
work plans:

B Pair work Change the Conversation Model, using the information on your notepad. Then change roles.

A: So what are you doing these days?

B: Well, ...

A: No kidding! I thought you had other plans.

B: That's right. I was going to . . . . , but . . . .

A: How come?

B: Well, ...

Don't stop!
• Discuss where you live and work now.
• Discuss other aspects of life: marriage, work, studies, children, or other topics.

C Change partners Practice the conversation again about other life choices and plans.

GOAL | **Express regrets about past actions**

GRAMMAR | *Perfect modals*

> **Use perfect modals to express thoughts about past actions.**
>
> **Express personal regret or judge another's actions: <u>should have</u> + past participle**
> I **should have studied** medicine. (But unfortunately, I didn't.)
> She **shouldn't have divorced** Sam. (But unfortunately, she did.)
>
> **Express possibility or speculate: <u>may have</u>, <u>might have</u> + past participle**
> I **may** (or **might**) **have failed** the final exam. It was really hard.
> He **may** (or **might**) **not have been** able to make a living as a painter.
>
> **Express certainty: <u>would have</u>, <u>could have</u> (for ability)**
> It's too bad he broke up with Anne. They **would have been** happy together.
> He was the driver. He **could have prevented** the accident.
>
> **Draw conclusions: <u>must have</u> + past participle**
> Beth isn't here. She **must have gone** home early.
> (I think that's what happened.)
> They didn't buy the house. The price **must not have been** acceptable.
> (I think that's the reason.)

> **GRAMMAR BOOSTER** ▶ p. 131
>
> *Regrets about the past:*
> • <u>Wish</u> + the past perfect
> • <u>Should have</u> and <u>ought to have</u>

Grammar practice Choose the modal that logically completes each sentence.
Write the modal and the verb in the perfect modal form.

1 I don't know why she married him. He .... the only man available.
(must / should) be

2 I .... architecture. I .... really good at it.
(should / may) study   (must / would) be

3 Jenna's not studying Chinese anymore. I guess it .... too hard to learn Chinese
(should / would) be
and Japanese at the same time.

4 We didn't know we were going to have five children. We .... such a small house.
(could not / should not) buy

5 Ella still loves Ben. She .... with him.
(must not / should not) break up

6 When I was young, everyone thought I was a great singer. But I decided to become a lawyer instead.
Looking back, I think I .... on the wrong career.
(may / should) decide

PRONUNCIATION | *Reduction of <u>have</u> in perfect modals*

3:24

A ◀)) Notice the reduction of <u>have</u> in perfect modals. Read and listen.
Then listen again and repeat.

/ʃʊdəv/
1 I should have married Marie.

/naɾəv/
3 We may not have seen it.

/maiɾəv/
2 They might have left.

/kʊdəv/
4 She could have been on time.

B Pair work Take turns reading the sentences with perfect modals in the
Grammar Practice above. Use correct reduction of <u>have</u>.

C Pair work Provide three possible reasons for each of the statements below. Use <u>may</u> / <u>might have</u>, <u>must have</u>, and <u>could have</u>. Follow the example.

Example: John is late for dinner.

1 My brother never got married.
2 All the classes were canceled today.
3 Michael is forty and he just became a doctor.
4 Rachel grew up in New York, but now she lives in São Paulo.
5 They had one child and then they adopted three more.
6 They had their honeymoon in the U.S. instead of in France.

"He might have gotten stuck in traffic."

"And he must not have taken his cell phone."

"Or he could have had an important meeting at work."

CONVERSATION MODEL

3:25

A 🔊 Read and listen to a conversation between two people discussing a regret about the past.

A: I should have married Steven.

B: Why do you think that?

A: Well, I might have had children by now.

B: Could be. But you never know. You might not have been happy.

A: True.

3:26

B 🔊 **Rhythm and intonation** Listen again and repeat. Then practice the Conversation Model with a partner.

NOW YOU CAN | Express regrets about past actions

A Notepadding Write about some regrets you have about past actions. Say how you think things might have been different in your life today.

Past action	Regret	How might things have been different?
a job / career choice	I didn't take the job at MacroTech.	I might have been CEO by now!

Past action	Regret	How might things have been different?
a job / career choice		
a field of study		
a marriage / divorce		
a boyfriend / girlfriend choice		
a breakup		

B Pair work Change the Conversation Model. Discuss your regrets and speculate on how things might have been different. Use information from your notepad and past modals. Then change roles.

A: I should (*or* I shouldn't) have ....

B: Why do you think that?

A: Well, I ....

B: Could be. But you never know. You might ....

A: ....

Don't stop!
• Ask your partner more questions about his or her regrets.
• Speculate about what happened.
• Offer advice.

♻ **Be sure to recycle this language.**

Why did you / didn't you ___ ?
Why don't you ___ ?
How about ___ ?

must (not) have
may / might (not) have
could have

BEFORE YOU LISTEN

A 🔊 3:27 **Vocabulary • *Skills and abilities*** Read and listen. Then listen again and repeat.

talents abilities in art, music, mathematics, etc., that you are born with
She was born with talents in both mathematics and art.

skills abilities that you learn, such as cooking, speaking a foreign language, or driving
She has several publishing skills: writing, editing, and illustrating.

experience time spent working at a job
Martin has a lot of experience in sales. He has worked at three companies.

knowledge understanding of or familiarity with a subject gained from experience or study
James has extensive knowledge of the history of film. You can ask him which classics to see.

B Think and explain Explain the following in your own words. Use examples from your life.

- the difference between a talent and a skill
- the difference between experience and knowledge

LISTENING COMPREHENSION

A 🔊 3:28 **Listen for details** Listen to nine people being interviewed at an international job fair. Stop after each interview and match the interviewee with his or her qualification for a job.

Interviewee		Qualifications	
..*h*..	**1** Sonia Espinoza	**a**	a good memory
......	**2** Silvano Lucastro	**b**	artistic ability
......	**3** Ivan Martinovic	**c**	mathematical ability
......	**4** Agnes Lukins	**d**	logical thinking
......	**5** Elena Burgess	**e**	compassion
......	**6** Karen Trent	**f**	manual dexterity
......	**7** Ed Snodgrass	**g**	common sense
......	**8** Akiko Uzawa	**h**	athletic ability
......	**9** Mia Kim	**i**	leadership skills

B Pair work With a partner, classify each qualification from Exercise A. Do you agree on all the classifications? Discuss and explain your opinions.

a talent	a skill
athletic ability	

> **❝** I think athletic ability is a talent. You're born with that. **❞**

> **❝** I don't agree. I think if you train and work at it, you can develop into a great athlete. I think it's a skill. **❞**

A Frame your ideas Take the skills inventory.

Careers, Jobs, Advanced Studies AND YOU

Whether you're looking for a job or interviewing for a school, interviewers expect you to answer questions about your interests, talents, skills, and experience. Take this inventory to prepare yourself for those questions.

Interests
Check the fields that interest you:
- ☐ business
- ☐ science
- ☐ education
- ☐ art
- ☐ manufacturing
- ☐ other _____

Qualifications
Check the qualifications you believe you have:
- ☐ manual dexterity
- ☐ logical thinking
- ☐ mathematical ability
- ☐ common sense
- ☐ athletic ability
- ☐ artistic ability
- ☐ compassion
- ☐ a good memory
- ☐ leadership skills
- ☐ other _____

Experience
Briefly note information about your experience, skills, and any special knowledge you have.

Experience: _____

Skills: _____

Special knowledge: _____

B Notepadding On your notepad, write specific examples of your qualifications. Then share and discuss your skills, abilities, and qualifications with a partner.

Qualification	Example
mathematical ability	I'm great at number puzzles.

Qualification	Example

C Pair work Use the information on your notepad to do one of the following activities.

- Role-play an interview for a job.
- Role-play an interview for career advice.
- Role-play an interview for entry into a professional (or other kind of) school.

D Group work Tell your class what you learned about your partner in the interview.

❝ My partner has a lot of experience in . . . ❞

♲ **Be sure to recycle this language.**

Interviewer
Please come in / have a seat.
Please tell me something about your [skills].
Do you have any knowledge of [Arabic]?
What kinds of [talents] do you have?
What [work] experience do you have?

Interviewee
I have experience in [teaching].
I don't have much experience, but ___ .
I'm good at [math].
I have three years of [French].

BEFORE YOU READ

A **Warm-up** How important do you think the following factors are to career success? Put the factors in order of importance. Make 1 the most important and 6 the least important.

☐ skills   ☐ talent   ☐ work habits

☐ prior experience   ☐ job knowledge   ☐ other ....

☐ physical appearance, dress, etc.

B **Discussion** Explain the reasons for your most important and least important choices. Use concrete examples.

READING 3:29

The Five Most Effective Work Habits
Advice to new workers from a CEO

If you are new to the working world, you are eager to demonstrate your skills and knowledge. However, in addition to those, some basic work habits may be even more effective in promoting your success. Read the following advice to new workers, written by the head of a company.

1 **Volunteer for assignments** One of the best ways to signal that you are a keen learner and are not afraid of hard work is to volunteer for assignments. However, before volunteering for a task, be sure you have the skills and knowledge to accomplish it successfully.

2 **Be nice to people** Be nice to people regardless of their rank or position. When you are nice to people, they go out of their way to help you, and every new worker needs help in order to get ahead.

3 **Prioritize your work** We all love to start work on things that are close to our hearts. However, these may not be the most urgent and important in our list of tasks to do.
    Have a list of things to do according to their strategic importance to your company. When you prioritize your work, you are more productive, and that increases your chances of career success.

4 **Stay positive** As someone new in the working world, you are not used to office culture. And there may be office politics that complicate things. Try to stay above politics and remain positive in the face of challenges. When you are positive, you stay focused on your goals. You make better decisions and, therefore, get more things done.

5 **Highlight a problem but bring solutions** Offer a solution each time you highlight a problem to your boss or management. You need to remember that when you bring problems and not solutions, people may think of you as a "complainer."

These five work habits, at first glance, may seem like common sense. However, in actual working environments, people tend to forget the basics. I counsel new workers in our company to internalize this behavior and consistently use it to increase their chances of career success.

Source: Adapted from www.career-success-for-newbies.com.

A Understand from context Find the words below in the article on page 70. Use context to help you write a definition for each. Then compare definitions with a partner.

a habit	
a solution	
volunteer	
prioritize	

B Confirm content Answer the following questions, according to what the CEO suggests.

1 Which is most important in determining a new worker's success: knowledge, work habits, or skills?

2 Why should workers volunteer to do tasks?

3 Why is "being nice" a valuable habit to develop?

4 What is the value of prioritizing tasks?

5 How does staying positive help you be more productive?

6 What's wrong with stating a problem without proposing a solution?

On your *ActiveBook* Self-Study Disc:
Extra Reading Comprehension Questions

NOW YOU CAN Discuss factors that promote success

A Notepadding On your notepad write some factors that have helped you be successful in your life, studies, or work, and some factors that have prevented you from being successful. (You can choose one, some, or all areas to comment on.) Then compare notepads with a partner.

Area	Factors that helped ☺	Factors that hurt ☹
my personal life	love, patience, common sense!	not listening to or paying attention to others

Area	Factors that helped ☺	Factors that hurt ☹
my personal life		
managing my home		
my studies / work		

B Discussion Discuss factors that you think promote success and factors that don't. Use your notepad for support, but expand on it with specific examples from your life to illustrate each factor. Talk about plans that changed and any regrets you may have.

♲ **Be sure to recycle this language.**

Qualities	Changes of plans	Regrets
talents	I thought I would ___ , but ___ .	I should have ___ .
skills	I was going to ___ , but ___ .	I could have ___ .
experience	I changed my mind.	I might have ___ .
knowledge	___ talked me out of it.	I would have ___ .
common sense	It's hard to make a living as ___ .	
	My tastes changed.	

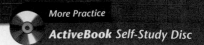

A 3:30 **Listening comprehension** Listen to the conversations between people talking about life changes. Write information on the notepad.

		Why did the person change his or her mind?	Any regrets?
	1		
	2		
	3		
	4		

B Explain the meaning of each of the following qualifications. Then write an occupation or course of study for a person with each qualification.

	Qualification	Definition	Occupation or Study
1	athletic ability		
2	artistic ability		
3	mathematical ability		
4	logical thinking ability		
5	a good memory		
6	leadership skills		

C Complete each statement of belief about the future, using <u>would</u>.

1 When I was a child, I thought I ....

2 My parents believed ....

3 My teachers were sure ....

4 When I finished school, I didn't know ....

D Read each sentence. On a separate sheet of paper, complete the statement in parentheses, using a perfect modal.

1 Marie was very unhappy in her marriage. (She should . . .)

2 After Sylvia and David got separated, they discovered they were still in love. (They could . . .)

	She should have tried to communicate
	more with her husband.

3 My parents were sorry they sold their country house. (They shouldn't . . .)

4 I can't understand how she learned to speak Italian so fast. (She might . . .)

5 Look at John's car. It's all smashed up. (He must . . .)

3:31/3:32
Top Notch Pop
"I Should Have Married Her"
Lyrics p. 150

E **Writing** Write a short autobiography. Include information about one or all of the topics below. If you have any regrets, express them, using past modals.

- your birth
- your childhood
- your studies
- other aspects of your life

WRITING BOOSTER ▸ p. 145

- *Dividing an essay into topics*
- *Guidance for Exercise E*

Story in pairs Choose one of the characters: Michael or Carlota. Look at the pictures for each of the three dates. Tell the story of your character to your partner. Then change partners and characters and tell the stories again.

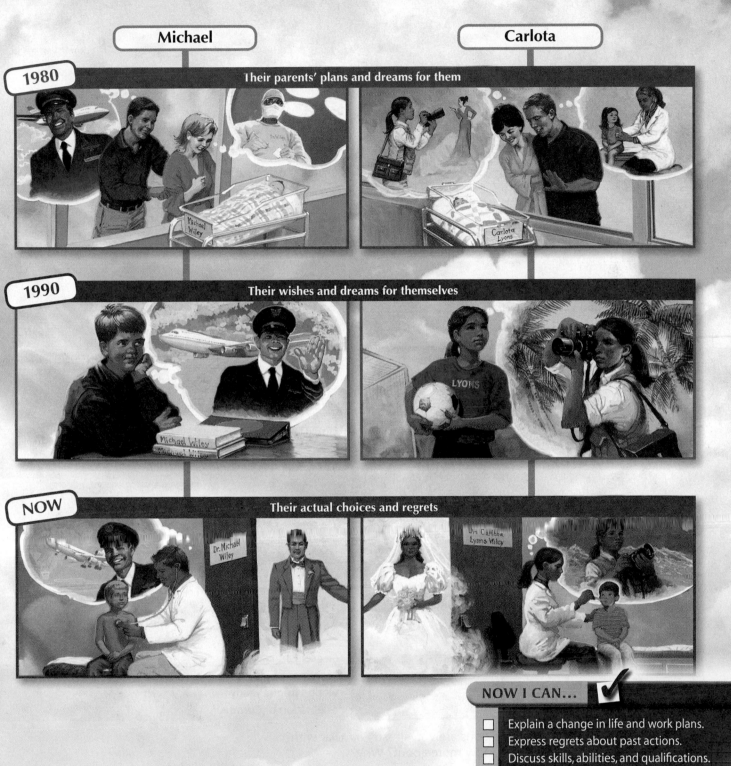

Michael

Carlota

1980 — Their parents' plans and dreams for them

1990 — Their wishes and dreams for themselves

NOW — Their actual choices and regrets

NOW I CAN...

☐ Explain a change in life and work plans.
☐ Express regrets about past actions.
☐ Discuss skills, abilities, and qualifications.
☐ Discuss factors that promote success.

Holidays and Traditions

GOALS | After Unit 7, you will be able to:

1 Wish someone a good holiday.
2 Ask about local customs.
3 Exchange information about holidays.
4 Explain wedding traditions.

United States

Thanksgiving dinner in the United States, featuring the traditional main dish of roast turkey

Japan

People picnicking and viewing the cherry blossoms at a *Hanami* party in Japan

Mexico

Friends who have come together for *Quinceañera* to celebrate a girl's fifteenth birthday and her entry into adulthood in Mexico

Korea

A couple dressed in the traditional hanbok during the Korean holiday of *Chuseok*

Brazil

Dancers in the fantastic costumes of Brazil's world-famous yearly celebration of *Carnaval*

A Look at the photos. Which traditions are you already familiar with? Which ones would you like to know more about? Why?

B **Discussion** Why do people think it's important to keep traditions alive? Do you think it's important to learn about the customs and traditions of other cultures? Explain your reasons.

C 🔊 4:02 **Photo story** Read and listen to a conversation about holiday traditions.

Basma: Wow! That dress your sister's wearing is gorgeous! What was the occasion?

Mi-Cha: Oh, that was for Chuseok. The dress is called a hanbok.

Basma: Did you say Chuseok? What's that—a holiday?

Mi-Cha: That's right. It's a traditional Korean holiday. It takes place in September or October each year to celebrate the harvest.

Basma: So does everyone dress up like that?

Mi-Cha: Some people do.

Basma: So what else does everyone do on Chuseok?

Mi-Cha: We get together with our relatives. And we eat a lot!

Basma: Well, that sounds nice.

Mi-Cha: Not only that, but we go to our hometowns and visit the graves of our ancestors.

Basma: So I suppose the airports and train stations are mobbed with people, right?

Mi-Cha: Totally. And the traffic is impossible. It takes hours to get anywhere.

Basma: I think every country's got at least one holiday like that!

Mi-Cha: What holiday comes to mind for you?

Basma: It reminds me of Eid al-Adha, a four-day religious holiday we celebrate where I come from.

Mi-Cha: In what way?

Basma: Well, people put on their best clothes, and we eat a ton of great food. We also travel to be with our relatives and visit the graves of our loved ones who have died.

Mi-Cha: How about that! Sounds just like our holiday.

Basma: Arabic speaker, Mi-Cha: Korean speaker

D Paraphrase Say each of the underlined expressions from the Photo Story in your <u>own</u> way.

1 It <u>takes place</u> in September or October.

....

2 We <u>get together with</u> our relatives.

....

3 The train stations are <u>mobbed with people</u>.

....

4 The traffic <u>is impossible</u>.

....

5 It <u>reminds me of</u> Eid al-Adha.

....

E Focus on language Write five sentences about a holiday or a tradition in your country, using the underlined language from Exercise D.

> Songkran takes place in April.

F Pair work Complete the chart about traditions in your country. Present your information to the class.

A special type of clothing	Explain when it is worn.
A type of music	Explain when it is played.
A special dish	Explain when it is eaten.
A traditional dance	Explain when it is danced.
A special event	Explain what happens.

ENGLISH FOR TODAY'S WORLD
connecting people from different cultures and language backgrounds

75

GOAL **Wish someone a good holiday**

CONVERSATION MODEL

A 🔊 4:03 Read and listen to a conversation about a holiday.

A: I heard there's going to be a holiday next week.

B: That's right. The Harvest Moon Festival.

A: What kind of holiday is it?

B: It's a seasonal holiday that takes place in autumn. People spend time with their families and eat moon cakes.

A: Well, have a great Harvest Moon Festival!

B: Thanks! Same to you!

4:05
🔊 **Types of holidays**
seasonal
historical
religious

B 🔊 4:04 **Rhythm and intonation** Listen again and repeat. Then practice the Conversation Model with a partner.

a moon cake

VOCABULARY   *Ways to commemorate a holiday*

A 🔊 4:06 Read and listen. Then listen again and repeat.

set off fireworks

march in parades

have picnics

pray

send cards

give each other gifts

wish each other well

remember the dead

wear costumes

B Pair work Match the Vocabulary with holidays and celebrations you know.

❝ Everyone wears costumes on . . . ❞

C 🔊 **Listening comprehension** Listen and use the Vocabulary to complete the chart.

	Type of holiday	What people do to celebrate
Mardi Gras (U.S.)		
Bastille Day (France)		
Tsagaan Sar (Mongolia)		

GRAMMAR *Adjective clauses with subject relative pronouns <u>who</u> and <u>that</u>*

Adjective clauses identify or describe people or things. Introduce adjective clauses about people with <u>who</u> or <u>that</u>.

A mariachi singer is someone	**who** (or **that**) **sings traditional Mexican music**.
Carnaval is a great holiday for people	**who** (or **that**) **like parades**.
Anyone	**who** (or **that**) **doesn't wear a costume** can't go to the festival.

Use <u>that</u>, not <u>who</u>, for adjective clauses that describe things.

Thanksgiving is a celebration	**that takes place in November**.
The parade	**that commemorates Bastille Day** is very exciting.

Be careful! Don't use a subject pronoun after the relative pronouns <u>who</u> or <u>that</u>.
  Don't say: Thanksgiving is a celebration that ~~it~~ takes place in November.

> **GRAMMAR BOOSTER** ▸ p. 131
> • *Adjective clauses: common errors*
> • *Reflexive pronouns*
> • *<u>By</u> + reflexive pronouns*
> • *Reciprocal pronouns: <u>each other</u> and <u>one another</u>*

A Understand the grammar Underline the adjective clauses and circle the relative pronouns.
Then draw an arrow from the relative pronoun to the noun or pronoun it describes.

1 Ramadan is a religious tradition that falls on a different day every year.

2 Chuseok is a Korean holiday that celebrates the yearly harvest.

3 The woman who designed our Halloween costumes for the parade was really talented.

4 The celebrations that take place in Brazil during Carnaval are a lot of fun.

5 People who celebrate April Fool's Day have a lot of fun every April 1st.

6 The Dragon Boat Festival in China is a celebration that takes place on the fifth day of the fifth moon, in May or June.

B Grammar practice On a separate sheet of paper, write five sentences with adjective clauses to describe some holidays and traditions in your country.

. . . is a religious tradition that . . .

. . . is a great holiday for people who . . .

NOW YOU CAN **Wish someone a good holiday**

A Pair work Use your holiday chart from page 75 to role-play the Conversation Model with a visitor to your country. Wish each other a good holiday. Then change roles.

A: I heard there's going to be a holiday next ....

B: That's right. ....

A: What kind of holiday is it?

B: It's a .... holiday that takes place in .... People ....

A: Well, have a .... !

B: Thanks! Same to you!

Some ways to exchange good wishes on holidays

Have a { nice / good / great / happy } [holiday]!

Enjoy yourself on [Chuseok]!
You too!
Same to you!

Don't stop!
Ask and answer more questions.
Use the Vocabulary.
  What else do people do?
  Do people ___ ?
  What kinds of ___ ?
  Where do people ___ ?

B Change partners Exchange wishes about other holidays.

GOAL   **Ask about local customs**

CONVERSATION MODEL

A 🔊 4:08 Read and listen to a conversation about local customs.

A: Do you mind if I ask you about something?

B: Of course not. What's up?

A: I'm not sure about the customs here. If someone invites you for dinner, should you bring the host a gift?

B: Yes. It's a good idea. But the gift that you bring should be inexpensive.

A: Would it be appropriate to bring flowers?

B: Definitely!

A: Thanks. That's really helpful.

B 🔊 4:09 **Rhythm and intonation** Listen again and repeat. Then practice the Conversation Model with a partner.

GRAMMAR   *Adjective clauses with object relative pronouns who, whom, and that*

In some adjective clauses, the relative pronoun is the subject of the clause.
The person **who comes for dinner** should bring a gift.
(who = subject / **The person** comes for dinner.)

In other adjective clauses, the relative pronoun is the object of the clause.
The person **who** (or **whom** or **that**) **you invite for dinner** should bring a gift.
(who = object / You invite **the person** for dinner.)

When the relative pronoun is the object of the clause, it may be omitted.
The person **you invite for dinner** should bring a gift.

Be careful!
When the relative pronoun is the subject of the clause, it can NOT be omitted.
Don't say: ~~The person comes for dinner~~ should bring a gift.
Do not use an object pronoun after the verb.
Don't say: The person who you invite ~~them~~ for dinner . . .

Relative pronouns
• Use <u>who</u> or <u>that</u> for a subject of a clause.
• Use <u>who</u>, <u>whom</u>, or <u>that</u> for an object of a clause.
Note: <u>Whom</u> is very formal.

GRAMMAR BOOSTER ▸ p. 133
• *Adjective clauses: who and whom in formal English*

A Understand the grammar Correct the error in the adjective clause in each sentence.
Explain each correction.

1 Putting butter on a child's nose is a birthday tradition ~~who~~ *that* people   " Only use <u>who</u> for people. "
observe on the Atlantic coast of Canada.

2 On the Day of the Dead, Mexicans remember family members who they have died.

3 The tomatoes that people throw them at each other during La Tomatina in Buñol, Spain, make a terrible mess.

4 The performer sang that traditional holiday song is world-famous.

5 The fireworks people set them off during the summer festivals in Japan are very beautiful.

B Grammar practice Complete the adjective clause in each sentence, using the cues. Omit the relative pronoun when possible.

1 People ……… *who visit other countries* ……… should find out the local customs.
     People visit other countries.

2 The man ……………………………………………… plays in a mariachi band.
                 You were talking with the man.

3 The young people ………………………………………… were all wearing
                       You saw the young people in the parade.
   traditional costumes.

4 The traditional Chinese dress ………………………………… is called a cheongsam.
                                 She's wearing the dress.

5 Anzac Day is a holiday …………………………………………… to remember
                         People celebrate the holiday in Australia.
   the soldiers who died in wars.

A Chinese woman wearing a traditional cheongsam

PRONUNCIATION   *"Thought groups"*

4:10

A 🔊 "Thought groups" clarify the meaning of sentences. Notice how sentence rhythm indicates how thoughts are grouped. Listen and repeat.

1 The person who comes for dinner should bring flowers.

2 The man we invited to the party is from Senegal.

3 The song that you were listening to is fado music from Portugal.

4 The Cherry Blossom Festival is a tradition that people observe in Japan every spring.

B Practice reading the sentences you completed in B Grammar Practice, breaking the sentences into thought groups.

NOW YOU CAN   Ask about local customs

A Pair work Change the Conversation Model. Role-play a conversation in which you ask about local customs. Use the ideas from the box below. Then change roles.

A: Do you mind if I ask you about something?

B: …… . What's up?

A: I'm not sure about the customs here. If ……… , should ……… ?

B: …… .

A: Would it be appropriate to ……… ?

B: …… .

A: Thanks. That's really helpful.

Ideas
• someone invites you out for dinner
• someone invites you to a party
• someone gives you a gift
• someone makes a special effort to help you
• your own idea:___

Don't stop!
Ask and answer other questions.
Is it OK if ___ ?
Would it be possible to ___ ?
Should I ___ ?

B Change partners Ask about local customs in other situations.

BEFORE YOU READ

Preview Look at the photos and the names of the holidays in the Reading. How would you categorize each holiday—historical, seasonal, or religious? Are you familiar with any of these holidays? What do you know about them?

READING 4:11

Holidays Around the World

Ramadan, the Month of Fasting

"May you be well throughout the year" is the typical greeting during Ramadan, the ninth month of the Islamic calendar, a special occasion for over one billion Muslims throughout the world. According to Islamic tradition, Ramadan marks the time when Muhammad received the word of God through the Koran. Throughout the month, Muslims fast—totally abstaining from food and drink from the break of dawn until the setting of the sun. It is also a time of increased worship and giving to the poor and the community. Ramadan ends with the festival of Eid ul-Fitr—three days of family celebrations—and eating!

Worshippers pray during Ramadan.

The Chinese New Year

The Chinese New Year is celebrated by Chinese around the world and marks the beginning of the first month in the Chinese calendar. The celebration usually takes place in February and lasts for fifteen days. Before the holiday begins, families clean out their houses to sweep away bad luck and they decorate their doors with red paper and big Chinese characters for happiness, wealth, and longevity. The night before, families gather together for a delicious meal. Outside, people set off firecrackers that make loud noises all through the night. In the morning, children wish their parents a healthy and happy new year and receive red envelopes with money inside. It is customary for people to give each other small gifts of fruits and sweets and to visit older family members. In the street, lion and dragon dancers set off more firecrackers to chase away evil spirits.

Dragon dancers chase away evil spirits.

Simón Bolívar's Birthday

Simón Bolívar was born on July 24, 1783 in Caracas, Venezuela. He is known throughout Latin America as "The Liberator" because of his fight for independence from Spain. He led the armies that freed Venezuela, Bolivia, Colombia, Ecuador, Peru, and Panama. He is memorialized in many ways, but two countries celebrate his birthday every July 24th—Venezuela and Ecuador. On that day, schools and most general businesses are closed and there are military parades and government ceremonies. But the malls are open and people usually use the holiday to go shopping.

Bolívar led the fight for independence

Sources: www.muhajabah.com and www.colostate.edu

A Scan for facts Complete the chart. Check the holidays on which each tradition is observed, according to the information in the Reading. Explain your answers.

On this holiday, people...	Bolívar's Birthday	Chinese New Year	Ramadan
give each other gifts.	○	○	○
wear costumes.	○	○	○
pray.	○	○	○
wish each other well.	○	○	○
get together with their families.	○	○	○
perform traditional dances.	○	○	○
decorate their homes.	○	○	○
celebrate for several days.	○	○	○
give away money.	○	○	○
have parades.	○	○	○
avoid eating during the day.	○	○	○

Which holiday is celebrated in more than one country?

○ Simón Bolívar's Birthday   ○ Chinese New Year   ○ Ramadan

B Compare and contrast Which holiday or traditions from the Reading do you find the most interesting? Why?

C Relate to personal experience Name one holiday you know for each tradition in the chart.

On your *ActiveBook* Self-Study Disc:
Extra Reading Comprehension Questions

NOW YOU CAN | Exchange information about holidays

A Notepadding With a partner, choose three holidays in your country. Discuss the traditions of each holiday and write notes about them on your notepads.

	A historical holiday	A seasonal holiday	A religious holiday
name of holiday			
purpose			
typical food			
typical music			
typical clothing			
other traditions			

B Group work Choose one of the holidays from your notepad and give an oral report to your classmates. Each student has to ask you one question.

♻ **Be sure to recycle this language.**

Traditionally, people ___ .	It's offensive to ___ .
It's customary to ___ .	___ is taboo.
It's probably best to ___ .	It's impolite to ___ .

GOAL | Explain wedding traditions

BEFORE YOU LISTEN

A 4:12 🔊 **Vocabulary** • *Getting married* Read and listen. Then listen again and repeat.

The events

an engagement an agreement to marry someone—**get engaged** *v.*

a (marriage) ceremony the set of actions that formally makes two single people become a married couple—**get married** *v.*

a wedding a formal marriage ceremony, especially one with a religious service

a reception a large formal party after a wedding ceremony

a honeymoon a vacation taken by two newlyweds after their wedding

The people

a fiancé a man who is engaged

a fiancée a woman who is engaged

a bride a woman at the time she gets married

a groom a man at the time he gets married

newlyweds the bride and groom immediately after the wedding

B Discussion Read about wedding traditions in many English-speaking countries. How are these similar or different from traditions practiced in your country?

The bride throws the bouquet after the wedding ceremony. The woman who catches it is believed to be the next to get married.

The newlyweds cut the cake together at the wedding reception.

The groom carries the bride "across the threshold," through the doorway to their new home. Soon after the wedding, they go on their honeymoon.

LISTENING COMPREHENSION

A 4:13 🔊 **Listen for the main idea** Listen to Part 1 of a lecture about a traditional Indian wedding. Which of the following statements best summarizes the information?

☐ **a** An Indian couple gets engaged long before the wedding.

☐ **b** There's a lot of preparation before an Indian wedding.

☐ **c** An Indian wedding lasts for days.

B 4:14 🔊 **Listen for details** Listen again to Part 1 and circle the best way to complete each statement.

1 A traditional Hindu wedding celebration can last for more than (two / five) days.

2 The bride's and groom's birthdates are used to choose the (engagement / wedding) date.

3 Before the wedding, musicians visit the (bride's / groom's) home.

4 The (bride / groom) is washed with oil.

5 An older relative offers the (bride / groom) money.

6 Relatives spend a lot of time painting the (bride's / groom's) skin.

C 🔊 **Listen for the main idea** Now listen to Part 2 of the lecture. What is the information mainly about?

☐ **a** the wedding ceremony　　☐ **b** the honeymoon　　☐ **c** the reception after the wedding

D 🔊 **Listen for details** Listen again to Part 2 and check the statements that are true. Correct the statements that are false.

☐ **1** Relatives wash the bride's and groom's hands.

☐ **2** The bride is seated behind a cloth so the groom cannot see her.

☐ **3** Relatives throw rice grains at the bride and groom.

☐ **4** The couple gives each other rings made of flowers.

☐ **5** The groom places a flower necklace around the bride's neck.

NOW YOU CAN　Explain wedding traditions

A **Frame your ideas** With a partner, read each saying or proverb about weddings and marriage. Discuss what you think each one means.

"The woman cries before the wedding and the man after."
Poland

"Marry off your son when you wish. Marry off your daughter when you can."
Italy

"Marriages are all happy. It's having breakfast together that causes all the trouble."
Ireland

"Marriage is just friendship if there are no children."
South Africa

Advice to the bride: "Wear something old and something new, something borrowed, and something blue."
United Kingdom

B **Discussion** Do you find any of the sayings or proverbs offensive? Why or why not? What sayings or proverbs about weddings do you know in your own language?

C **Notepadding** On your notepad, make a list of wedding traditions in your country. Compare your lists with those of other groups.

D **Pair work** Role-play a conversation in which you describe local wedding traditions to a visitor to your country. Ask and answer questions about the details.

❝ So how does a couple get engaged here? ❞

❝ Well, before they get engaged, they have to . . . ❞

Before the wedding:
At the wedding ceremony:
After the wedding:

More Practice
ActiveBook Self-Study Disc

grammar · vocabulary · listening
reading · speaking · pronunciation

A 🔊 4:17 **Listening comprehension** Listen to each conversation and circle the occasion or the people they are talking about. Then circle T if the statement is true or F if it is false. Correct any false statements.

1	an engagement / a reception / a honeymoon	**T F**	The man who is speaking is the groom.
2	an engagement / a reception / a honeymoon	**T F**	The man who is speaking is the groom.
3	a bride / a groom / relatives	**T F**	The woman who is speaking is the bride.
4	a bride / a groom / relatives	**T F**	The woman who is speaking is a guest.

B Complete each statement, using the unit Vocabulary. Then write the name of a holiday or celebration you know for each statement.

Name a holiday when people . . .	Examples
1 .... fireworks.	
2 .... in parades.	
3 .... picnics.	
4 .... time with their families.	
5 wear	
6 give .... gifts.	
7 .... other well.	

4:18/4:19
🎵 *Top Notch Pop*
"Endless Holiday"
Lyrics p. 150

C Complete each sentence with an adjective clause.

1 A groom is a man *who has just gotten married* ....

2 Eid al-Adha is a religious holiday ....

3 A honeymoon is a vacation ....

4 A hanbok is a traditional dress ....

5 A wedding reception is a party ....

6 Chuseok is a holiday ....

D On a separate sheet of paper, answer each question in your <u>own</u> way.

1 What's your favorite holiday? What kind of holiday is it (seasonal, historical, religious)?

2 What's the longest holiday in your country? How long is it?

3 What's the most interesting wedding tradition in your country?

> *My favorite holiday is Semana Santa. It's a religious holiday that takes place for a week in March or April.*

E **Writing** On a separate sheet of paper, describe two different holidays that are celebrated in your country. Include as many details as you can about each.

- What kind of holiday is it?
- When is it celebrated?
- How is it celebrated?
- What do people do / eat / say / wear, etc.?

WRITING BOOSTER ▸ p. 146

- *Descriptive details*
- *Guidance for Exercise E*

Pair work challenge For one minute, look at the photos and Fact Sheet for one of the holidays. Your partner looks at the other holiday. Then close your books. Ask and answer questions about each other's holidays. For example:

Why do people celebrate Songkran?

Pair work Create conversations for the people.

1 Ask about one of the holidays. Start like this:
I heard there's going to be a holiday.

2 Ask about local customs during the holiday. Start like this:
Do you mind if I ask you something?

Group presentation Choose one of the holidays and give a presentation to your group or class. Use adjective clauses.
Songkran is a seasonal holiday that . . .

Songkran Water Festival

Celebrated in Thailand. Lasts for three days.

Marks the . . .
- *start of the Buddhist New Year.*
- *beginning of the farming season.*

People . . .
- *clean their homes.*
- *make offerings at temples.*
- *sing and dance in the street.*
- *throw lots of water at each other!*

NOTE: *Don't worry! It's customary for people to throw lots of water at complete strangers on this holiday.*

Mexican Independence Day

Celebrated on September 15 and 16.

Commemorates . . .
- *the beginning of the War of Independence.*
- *Mexico's independence from Spain.*

People . . .
- *march in parades.*
- *perform traditional music and dances.*
- *decorate with the colors of the Mexican flag (red, white, and green).*
- *set off fireworks.*
- *eat special dishes (sometimes red, white, and green).*

NOTE: *It's customary for people to shout, "Viva México!" Even if you are not Mexican, you can join in.*

NOW I CAN... ✔

- ☐ Wish someone a good holiday.
- ☐ Ask about local customs.
- ☐ Exchange information about holidays.
- ☐ Explain wedding traditions.

Inventions and Discoveries

the wheel

the steam locomotive

the mosquito net

penicillin: the first "wonder drug"

28 Tablets

28 PENICILLIN V TABLETS
Take ONE FOUR times

Pe
(Phe)

the automobile

the television

A Discussion Most of the pictures represent inventions. Do you know which one resulted from a discovery? How would you explain the difference between an invention and a discovery? Provide some examples of inventions and discoveries.

B ◀))) **Photo story** Read and listen to a conversation about how an invention might have helped someone.

Leslie: This itching is driving me crazy!

Jody: Look at your arm! Are those mosquito bites?

Leslie: Yeah. Ben and I got eaten alive last weekend. We went away for a second honeymoon at this cute little bed and breakfast in the mountains, but the mosquitoes were brutal.

Jody: That doesn't sound very romantic. Didn't they have screens in the windows?

Leslie: Well, they did, but ours had a big hole and we didn't realize it until the middle of the night. What a nightmare!

Jody: Too bad you didn't bring any insect repellent. There are tons of mosquitoes in the mountains this time of year. Hello?

Leslie: We actually did have some, but it just didn't work that well. You know how Ben is—everything has to be organic and natural.

Jody: Well, with all due respect to Ben, you just have to bite the bullet once in a while and use the stuff that works. Whether you like it or not, the poison is effective.

Leslie: I agree, but Ben won't hear of it. You know, next time we go away for a romantic weekend, I'm packing one of those mosquito nets to hang over the bed.

C Paraphrase Say each of the underlined expressions from the Photo Story in your own way.

1 "Ben and I got eaten alive last weekend."

2 ". . . the mosquitoes were brutal."

3 "What a nightmare!"

4 "There are tons of mosquitoes in the mountains this time of year."

5 ". . . you just have to bite the bullet once in a while and use the stuff that works."

6 "I agree, but Ben won't hear of it."

7 ". . . I'm packing one of those mosquito nets to hang over the bed."

D Think and explain Answer the following questions, according to the Photo Story.

1 What effect does a mosquito bite cause?

2 Where were Leslie and Ben when they got the mosquito bites?

3 How did mosquitoes get into their bedroom?

4 Why would Ben object to "the stuff that works"?

5 What is another preventive measure against mosquitoes?

E Opinion survey Rank the inventions and discoveries in order of importance from 1 (most important) to 10 (least important). Explain the reason for ranking one the most important.

Rank	Item	Rank	Item
	air travel		pasteurization of milk products
	antibiotics		the Internet
	cell phones		vaccination
	insect repellents		water purification systems
	mosquito nets		other:

GOAL Describe technology

VOCABULARY Describing manufactured products

A 🔊 4:21 Read and listen. Then listen again and repeat.

Uses new technology		Offers high quality		Uses new ideas	
high-tech	OR	high-end	OR	innovative	OR
state-of-the-art	OR	top-of-the-line	OR	revolutionary	OR
cutting-edge		first-rate		novel	

B 🔊 4:22 **Listening comprehension** Listen to the ads. Choose the correct word or phrase to describe the product.

1 The Strawberry smart phone is (state-of-the-art / top-of-the-line).

2 The Blackstone is a (revolutionary / high-end) device.

3 The Micro Scanner is a (high-end / cutting-edge) product.

4 The Digicon B1X Beta is a (novel / first-rate) camera.

5 The 17-inch LCD Monitor is (innovative / top-of-the-line).

GRAMMAR Conditional sentences: review

> **GRAMMAR BOOSTER** ▸ p. 134
> - *Real and unreal conditionals: review*
> - *Clauses after <u>wish</u>*
> - *<u>Unless</u> in conditional sentences*

Real (or "factual") conditionals	Unreal conditionals
If you **want** a fuel-efficient car, you **need** something smaller. If you **buy** the Alva, you**'ll get** great fuel efficiency and a top-of-the-line car. **Remember: Never use a future form in the <u>if</u>- clause.** Don't say: If you ~~will buy~~ the Alva . . .	If I **were** you, I **wouldn't buy** the Digicom. (unreal: I'm not you.) If Blueberry **had** a cutting-edge smart phone, it **would outsell** Strawberry. (unreal: It doesn't.) **Remember: Never use <u>would</u> in the <u>if</u>- clause.** Don't say: If Blueberry ~~would have~~ . . .

A Understand the grammar Check the statements that describe unreal conditions.

☐ 1 If they see something first-rate, they buy it.

☐ 2 If we take the bus to town, we save a lot of time.

☐ 3 If you turned off your cell phone in the theater, it wouldn't bother the other theatergoers.

☐ 4 If I rent the Alva, I'll save a bundle of money on gas.

☐ 5 They won't be able to upload the photos if they don't have a good Internet connection.

☐ 6 If she were here, she would explain how to use the Digicon remote telephone.

☐ 7 If the doctor prescribed an antibiotic, I would take it.

B Grammar practice Choose the correct form.

1 If the Teknicon 17-inch monitor (were / would be) on sale, I (will / would) buy it right away.

2 Most people (buy / will buy) state-of-the-art products if they (have / will have) enough money.

3 If they (would invent / invented) a safe way to text-message while driving, people (will / would) be very happy.

4 If she (knew / would know) about the Pictopia phone camera, she (uses / would use) it on her next work assignment.

5 If I (have / will have) an Internet connection in my hotel room, I (send / will send) you the report by tomorrow morning.

6 What (will / would) you do if your laptop (breaks / will break)?

7 I (won't / wouldn't) buy a Lunetti phone if I (have / had) all the money in the world. No one needs such a high-end phone in the office.

C Grammar practice With a partner, complete each statement with an *if*- clause or a result clause. Then share and explain some statements with your class.

1 If money were not a problem, . . .

2 People would stop getting infected with diseases if . . .

3 If people are not careful when they choose new products, . . .

4 I would stay up all night tonight if . . .

CONVERSATION MODEL

4:23

A 🔊 Read and listen to a conversation about new technology.

A: I just got a new car.

B: No kidding! What kind?

A: The Alva 500. The 500 model is top-of-the-line. I thought I'd treat myself.

B: Well, congratulations! If I had the money, I'd get a new car myself.

4:24

B 🔊 **Rhythm and intonation** Listen again and repeat. Then practice the Conversation Model with a partner.

NOW YOU CAN   Describe technology

A Notepadding Write one product you've recently gotten (or would like to have) for each category.

Quality	Product name	Adjective
Uses new technology:	the Whisper combination hairdryer / cell phone	state-of-the-art

Quality	Product name	Adjective
Uses new technology:		
Offers high quality:		
Uses new ideas:		

B Pair work Role-play a new conversation, changing the Conversation Model with one of the products and adjectives on your notepads. Use the unreal conditional. Then change roles.

A: I just got ....

B: No kidding! What kind?

A: .... It's .... I thought I'd treat myself.

B: Well, congratulations! If I .... , I'd ....

C Change partners Personalize the conversation again, using other products on your notepads.

Don't stop!

Discuss another product and use other adjectives. Ask questions about it:
• What does it look like?
• How does it work?
• How fast / accurate / powerful is it?
• Does it work well?
• Is it guaranteed?

LESSON 2

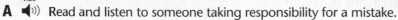

GOAL Take responsibility for a mistake

CONVERSATION MODEL

A 🔊 4:25 Read and listen to someone taking responsibility for a mistake.

A: Sorry I'm late. I thought the meeting was tomorrow.

B: What happened?

A: I'm ashamed to say I just forgot to put it on my calendar.

B: Don't worry. That can happen to anyone.

A: Well, if I had written it down, I wouldn't have forgotten.

B: No harm done. We were just getting started.

B 🔊 4:26 **Rhythm and intonation** Listen again and repeat.
Then practice the Conversation Model with a partner.

GRAMMAR *The past unreal conditional*

The past unreal conditional describes unreal or untrue conditions and results.
Use the past perfect in the **if-** clause. Use <u>would</u> **have** or <u>could</u> **have** in the result clause.

If she **had rented** a more economical car, she **wouldn't have spent** so much money on gas. (unreal condition: She <u>didn't</u> rent a more economical car.)

If Jonas Salk **hadn't invented** a vaccine to protect people against polio, many more people **would have gotten** the disease. (unreal condition: He <u>did</u> invent a vaccine.)

Questions and answers

Could they **have prevented** the accident if they **had known** the tires were so old?
(Yes, they **could have.** / No, they **couldn't have.**)

How many people **would have been injured or killed** if air bags **hadn't been invented**? (No one knows exactly, but a lot.)

> **Be careful!**
> Don't use <u>would</u> or <u>could</u> in the **if-** clause.
> Don't say: "If Jonas Salk ~~wouldn't have~~ invented…"

> **GRAMMAR BOOSTER** ▸ p. 135
> *The unreal conditional: variety of forms*

A **Understand the grammar** Choose the meaning of each past unreal conditional sentence.

1 I wouldn't have gone to class if I had known I had the flu.
  a I went to class.   **b** I didn't go to class.

2 If we had used our GPS, we wouldn't have gotten lost.
  a We got lost.   **b** We didn't get lost.

3 If they hadn't planted those new genetically engineered tomatoes, they would have lost this year's crop.
  a They lost this year's crop.   **b** They didn't lose this year's crop.

4 The airline wouldn't have canceled the flight if they hadn't had a program to predict engine failure.
  a They canceled the flight.   **b** They didn't cancel the flight.

B **Grammar practice** Choose the correct forms to complete each past unreal conditional sentence.

1 What .... you .... if you .... a phone in your car?
                 do   not / have

2 We .... this digital video conference if an Internet connection .... available.
        cannot / have   not / be

3 If our old film camera .... , we .... this digital one.
                       not / break   not / buy

4 If she .... her smart phone with GPS, she .... late for the dinner.
         take   would not / be

5 If instrument navigation .... , intercontinental air travel ....
                    not / be invented   not / develop

C Grammar practice

With a partner, take turns reading each situation and completing each statement. Use the past unreal conditional. More than one answer is possible.

1 On Monday you bought a new Blendini sports car because its advertising said it was very economical. However, you didn't check the facts. Then on Friday you saw an article in the newspaper: "Blendini Company fined for lying about statistics. Car uses more fuel than all others of its class."

If I had seen ....
....

2 You forgot to close the windows in your house before a weekend trip. There was a terrible rainstorm. When you got home, some of your furniture was damaged by the water. Your family blamed you because you were the last to leave the house.

If I hadn't forgotten ....
....

3 There was a big sale at the Morton Street Mall. Everything in every store was half-price. You didn't know and you went shopping somewhere else. When you got home, a friend called to tell you about all the bargains she got.

If I ....
....

4 You bought some insect repellent for a trip to the mountains. When you got there, the mosquitoes were brutal. Before you sprayed the repellent on yourself and your children, you looked at the label. It said, "Caution. Not for use on children under 12."

If I ....
....

PRONUNCIATION Contractions with 'd in spoken English

A 🔊 **4:27** Notice the reduction of <u>had</u>, <u>would</u>, and <u>did</u>. Read and listen. Then listen again and repeat.

1 Where did you go? → /wɛrd/ **Where'd** you go?*   **3** It would be OK. → /ɪtəd/ **It'd** be OK.*

2 Who did you see? → /hud/ **Who'd** you see?*   **4** If we had had a map, we wouldn't have gotten lost. → /wid/ If **we'd** had a map, we wouldn't have gotten lost.

* **Note:** <u>Where'd</u>, <u>Who'd</u>, and <u>It'd</u> are contracted in speech, but not in writing.

B 🔊 **4:28** **Listening comprehension** Write the sentences you hear. Write full, not contracted, forms.

1 ....   4 ....

2 ....   5 ....

3 ....   6 ....

NOW YOU CAN Take responsibility for a mistake

A Pair work Change the Conversation Model. Role-play a conversation, taking responsibility for a mistake. Use the ideas (or your own mistake and reason) and the past unreal conditional. Then change roles.

A: Sorry I ....

B: What happened?

A: I'm ashamed to say I just ....

B: Don't worry. That can happen to anyone.

A: Well, if I had .... , I .... have ....

B: No harm done. ....

B Change partners Take responsibility for another mistake.

Ideas

Some mistakes you can make
• You were late for something.
• You forgot to do something.
• You missed a meeting.
• You missed someone's birthday.
• You didn't call someone.
• You didn't return someone's call.

Some reasons for a mistake
• You accidentally deleted an e-mail.
• You forgot to write something down.
• You wrote down the wrong date or time.
• You just got too busy and it slipped your mind.
• You had an emergency.

BEFORE YOU LISTEN

A ◀))) **Vocabulary** • *More descriptive adjectives* Read and listen. Then listen again and repeat.
4:29

| low-tech / high-tech | wacky | unique | efficient / inefficient |

B Complete the chart with the correct adjective and one product or invention you know.

Definition	Adjective	A product or invention
the only one of its kind		
pretty silly		
doesn't use modern technology		
uses modern technology		
doesn't waste time, money, or energy		
wastes time, money, or energy		

LISTENING COMPREHENSION

A ◀))) **Listen for main ideas** Listen and then write each problem in your own words.
4:30

1 .... 3 ....

2 .... 4 ....

B ◀))) **Listen to associate** Listen again and write the number of the conversation next to
4:31
the invention each person should have had.

☐

☐

☐

☐

C **Discussion** Describe each of the inventions. Use
one or more of the adjectives from the Vocabulary
above and from page 88.

> ❝ It's not a novel idea, but the Pet Exit
> is both low-tech and efficient. It
> doesn't need electronics or machinery. ❞

A Frame your ideas Check the boxes to show where you think new inventions are needed. Then complete the chart with ideas.

	New invention needed	Benefit of the invention
At home and in the car		
☑ for safety in the car	*a wake-up alarm*	*so you don't fall asleep while driving*

	New invention needed	Benefit of the invention
At home and in the car		
☐ for safety in the car		
☐ for safety at home		
☐ for organizing things		
☐ for cooking and preparing food		
☐ for raising children		
☐ for taking care of pets		
☐ for relaxing		
In the office		
☐ for writing		
☐ for organizing papers		
☐ for training staff		
☐ for communicating		
☐ for eating lunch or snacking		
In English class		
☐ for learning new words		
☐ for learning grammar		
☐ for getting more speaking practice		
☐ for preparing to take tests		

B Project In small groups, discuss and choose one invention from someone's chart. Give the invention a name. (The invention can be low-tech, high-tech, wacky, or even impossible! The name can be funny.) Draw a picture of the invention. Then write an advertisement for your invention. Include real and unreal conditional sentences in your ad.

 Be sure to recycle this language.

top-of-the-line	wacky
high-tech / low-tech	practical
high-end	unique
state-of-the-art	efficient / inefficient
cutting-edge	novel
first-rate	revolutionary
innovative	

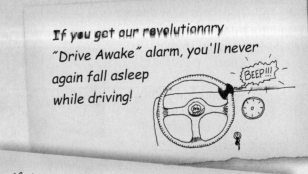

If you get our revolutionary "Drive Awake" alarm, you'll never again fall asleep while driving!

BEEP!!!

If she had brought the state-of-the-art "EAR-RINGS," she would have gotten your phone call.

Hello?

C Group work Present your ads to the class.

BEFORE YOU READ

Warm-up Of the following inventions that help people communicate in words, which do you think was the most important: the printing press, the telephone, the radio, the television, or the Internet? Explain your opinion.

READING 4:32

The Printing Press

Until the 6th or 7th century, all books had to be written by hand.

If you asked a large number of people what the most important invention has been, many would say the wheel. But many others would say the printing press. It's debatable which altered history more. But without a doubt, the printing press ranks within the top two or three inventions in history.

Long before the telephone, the television, the radio, and the computer, the written word was the only way to communicate ideas to people too far away to talk with. Until the sixth or seventh century, all books had to be written by hand. For that reason, very few books existed and, therefore, very few people read them.

In the sixth and seventh centuries, the Japanese and Chinese invented a way to print pages by carving characters and pictures on wooden, ivory, or clay blocks. They would put ink on a block and then press paper onto the ink, printing a page from the block. This process is called letterpress printing. The invention of letterpress printing was a great advance in communication because each block could be inked many times and many copies of each page could be made. Many books could now be made. Therefore, many people could read the same book.

Later, in the eleventh century, another great advance occurred. The Chinese invented "movable" type. Each character was made as a separate block which could be used many times in many texts. This meant that pages could be created by putting together these individual characters rather than having to have each whole page carved. Movable type was much more efficient than the earlier Japanese and Chinese print blocks because books could be created much more quickly by people with less skill.

In Europe, movable type was used for the first time in the fifteenth century. And there, Johannes Gutenberg invented typecasting, a way to make movable type much more quickly, by melting metal and pouring it into the forms of the letters. This greatly increased the speed of printing because letters could now be used more than one time on a page. Eventually, movable type made books available to many more people.

A ladle for pouring hot metal

Carved print blocks

Information source: Eyewitness Books: *Invention.* By Lionel Bender, Alfred A. Knopf, New York, © 1991.

A **Infer information** Answer the following questions in your <u>own</u> words, using information from the Reading.

1 What modern forms of communication don't depend on the "written word"?

2 Why were there so few books before the invention of printing?

3 What's the difference between letterpress printing and printing using movable type?

4 What advantages did movable type have over letterpress printing?

5 How would you describe Gutenberg's invention?

6 How did typecasting improve the process of printing?

B **Identify cause and effect** Discuss these questions. Use the conditional when possible.

1 If typecasting hadn't been invented, how would ideas have traveled great distances prior to the invention of the telephone?

2 If the printing press hadn't been invented, how would the world be different today?

On your *ActiveBook* Self-Study Disc:
Extra Reading Comprehension Questions

NOW YOU CAN | Discuss the impact of inventions/discoveries

A **Frame your ideas** Look at some key inventions and discoveries and how they changed people's lives.

2000 B.C.E.: The plow loosens and turns the soil so crops can be planted efficiently.

1796: The discovery by Edward Jenner of the process of vaccination made the first successful vaccine possible.

1914: The modern zipper permits the opening and closing of clothes without buttons and buttonholes.

1940–1945: The first electronic computers, the size of a large room, manipulated data according to a set of instructions. The computer opened a new era of communications and research technology.

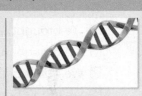

1953: James Watson, Francis Crick, and Rosalind Franklin clarified the basic structure of DNA, the genetic material for expressing life in all its forms. This discovery made the possibilities of genetic engineering practical for the first time.

B **Notepadding** Write your ideas about how life was before and after each invention or discovery.

	Life before	Life after
the plow		
vaccination		
the zipper		
the computer		
the DNA molecule		

Text-mining (optional):
Underline language in the Reading on page 94 to help you with your report. For example:
"Before ___, ___ was the only way to ..."

C **Group report** Present a report about an invention or a discovery to your class. Describe its impact in history. Use the past unreal conditional.

" After the plow was invented, farmers could plant large areas. If it hadn't been invented, they couldn't have planted enough food to sell. "

Review

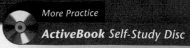
A ◀)) **Listening comprehension** Listen to people talking about new products. Match the name of each product with the best adjective to describe it.

Name of product	Adjective
___ 1 The Ultraphone	**a** top-of-the-line
___ 2 Dinner-from-a-distance	**b** unique
___ 3 Kinder-TV	**c** efficient
___ 4 Ten Years Off	**d** cutting-edge

B Check the statement that is true for each situation.

1 We wouldn't have gotten lost if we had remembered to bring our portable GPS device.

☐ We brought it, and we got lost.

☐ We brought it, and we didn't get lost.

☐ We didn't bring it, and we got lost.

☐ We didn't bring it, and we didn't get lost.

2 If the salesclerk were here, she would explain how the Omni works.

☐ The salesclerk is here, so she will explain how the Omni works.

☐ The salesclerk is here, but she won't explain how the Omni works.

☐ The salesclerk isn't here, but she will explain how the Omni works.

☐ The salesclerk isn't here, so she won't explain how the Omni works.

3 If Ron had bought the Ultraphone, he would already have sent those e-mails.

☐ Ron bought the Ultraphone, and he has already sent those e-mails.

☐ Ron bought the Ultraphone, but he hasn't sent those e-mails yet.

☐ Ron didn't buy the Ultraphone, but he has already sent those e-mails.

☐ Ron didn't buy the Ultraphone, so he hasn't sent those e-mails yet.

4:34/4:35
🎵 **Top Notch Pop**
"Reinvent the Wheel"
Lyrics p. 150

C Complete each conditional sentence.

1 If the computer hadn't been invented, ...

2 If I had to decide what the most important scientific discovery in history was, ...

....

3 If most people cared about the environment, ...

4 If gasoline, heating oil, and other products that come from fossil fuels become scarce, ...

....

5 If I could invent an inexpensive yet innovative low-tech solution to a problem, ...

....

D **Writing** Choose one of the following inventions: the car, the television, or the Internet, or another invention. On a separate sheet of paper, describe the advantages, disadvantages, and historical impact of the invention you chose.

WRITING BOOSTER ▸ p. 146

• Summary statements
• Guidance for Exercise D

Uses of the Wheel

logs used as wheels

two-wheeled carts

a horse-drawn chariot

a wooden wagon wheel

a potter's wheel

an automobile

Contest Look at the pictures about the uses of the wheel for one minute. Then close your books and try to remember all the uses of the wheel in the pictures. You get a bonus point for thinking of another use.

Pair work

1 Choose one use of the wheel. Discuss how it changed history and people's lives. Present your ideas. For example:

> The log helped people move heavy objects over great distances. They could build more easily with stone.

2 The family in the second picture is late. Create a conversation for the two women. Start like this:

> A: Hello, Mom. I'm sorry. We're going to be late. If . . .

NOW I CAN...

- ☐ Describe technology.
- ☐ Take responsibility for a mistake.
- ☐ Describe how inventions solve problems.
- ☐ Discuss the impact of inventions/discoveries.

97

Controversial Issues

GOALS **After Unit 9, you will be able to:**
1 Bring up a controversial subject.
2 Discuss controversial issues politely.
3 Propose solutions to global problems.
4 Debate the pros and cons of issues.

How politically literate are you?

Test yourself to find out.

Choose the correct term for each definition. Then look at the answers to see how you did.

1 The group of people who govern a country or state
  ⭕ a government   ⭕ a constitution

2 The art or science of government or governing
  ⭕ a constitution   ⭕ politics

3 A set of basic laws and principles that a country is governed by, which cannot easily be changed by the political party in power
  ⭕ a constitution   ⭕ a democracy

4 An occasion when people vote to choose someone for an official position
  ⭕ a government   ⭕ an election

5 Show by marking a paper or using a machine, etc., which person you want in a government position
  ⭕ govern   ⭕ vote

6 Lead or take part in a series of actions intended to win an election for a government position
  ⭕ campaign   ⭕ vote

7 A system of government in which every citizen in the country can vote to elect its government officials
  ⭕ a monarchy   ⭕ a democracy

8 The system in which a country is ruled by a king or queen
  ⭕ a dictatorship   ⭕ a monarchy

9 Government by a ruler who has complete power
  ⭕ a democracy   ⭕ a dictatorship

10 A country ruled by a king or a queen whose power is limited by a constitution
  ⭕ a dictatorship   ⭕ a constitutional monarchy

ANSWERS: 1 a government 2 politics 3 a constitution 4 an election 5 vote 6 campaign 7 a democracy 8 a monarchy 9 a dictatorship 10 a constitutional monarchy

---

A 🔊 5:02 **Vocabulary • *Political terminology*** Read and listen. Then listen again and repeat.

| a government | a constitution | vote | a democracy | a dictatorship |
| politics | an election | campaign | a monarchy | a constitutional monarchy |

B **Pair work** How much do you know about world politics? On the chart, discuss and write the name of at least one country for each type of government. Then compare charts with other classmates.

A democracy	A monarchy	A constitutional monarchy	A dictatorship

C 5:03 🔊)) **Photo story** Read and listen to a conversation about discussing politics.

ENGLISH FOR TODAY'S WORLD
connecting people from different cultures
and language backgrounds

San-Chi: So what are you up to these days, Sam?

Sam: Hi, San-Chi! What a coincidence. I've been meaning to give you a call. I need some cultural advice.

San-Chi: What about?

Sam: Well, I'm having dinner at Mei-Li's house tonight, and her parents are in from Taiwan.

San-Chi: Really?

Sam: Mm-hmm. And you know how much I love to talk politics. Would it be rude to bring that up at the dinner table?

San-Chi: Uh . . . Well, not really. Most people from Taiwan like to talk about politics, too. But it would not be cool to argue with them if you don't agree with what they say.

Sam: How well you know me! I do tend to be a little opinionated.

San-Chi: Well, in that case, I'd advise you to talk about something else!

San-Chi: Chinese speaker

D Paraphrase Say each of the following statements from the Photo Story in your <u>own</u> way.

1 "So what are you up to these days, . . .?"
2 "I've been meaning to give you a call."
3 "Would it be rude to bring that up at the dinner table?"
4 ". . . it would not be cool to argue with them . . ."
5 "I do tend to be a little opinionated."

E Think and explain Answer the following questions, based on the Photo Story.

1 Why does Sam say, "What a coincidence" when San-Chi greets him?
2 Why does Sam choose San-Chi to ask his cultural question?
3 Why do you think Sam is concerned about the dinner-table conversation at Mei-Li's house?
4 Why does San-Chi suggest Sam talk about something other than politics at Mei-Li's?

F Discussion

1 Do you like to talk about politics? Do you think politics is a good topic for discussion when you are invited to someone's home? Explain.

2 Review the types of government from page 98. Do you think every country should have the same form of government? Why don't all countries have the same form of government? In your opinion, is there a "best" form of government? Explain.

Do you like to discuss politics at the dinner table?

GOAL | **Bring up a controversial subject**

VOCABULARY | *A continuum of political and social beliefs*

A 🔊 5:04 Read and listen. Then listen again and repeat.

radical *adj.* supporting complete political or social change —**a radical** *n.*

liberal *adj.* supporting changes in political, social, or religious systems that respect the different beliefs, ideas, etc., of other people —**a liberal** *n.*

moderate *adj.* having opinions or beliefs, especially about politics, that are not extreme and that most people consider reasonable or sensible —**a moderate** *n.*

conservative *adj.* preferring to continue to do things as they have been done in the past rather than risking changes —**a conservative** *n.*

reactionary *adj.* strongly opposed to political or social change —**a reactionary** *n.*

B 🔊 5:05 **Listening comprehension** Listen to each conversation. Then, with a partner, complete the chart. Listen again if necessary to check your work or settle any disagreements.

	radical	liberal	moderate	conservative	reactionary
1 He's	○	○	○	○	○
2 She's	○	○	○	○	○
3 He's	○	○	○	○	○
4 She's	○	○	○	○	○
5 He's	○	○	○	○	○

CONVERSATION MODEL

A 🔊 5:06 Read and listen to a conversation about politics.

A: Do you mind if I ask you a political question? I hope it's not too personal.

B: No problem. What would you like to know?

A: Well, are you a liberal or a conservative?

B: Actually, I'm neither. I like to make up my mind based on the issue.

A: So would you say you're an independent?

B: I guess you could say that.

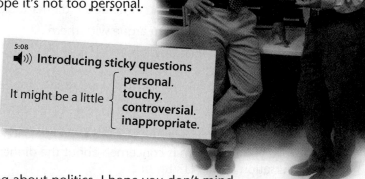

🔊 5:08 **Introducing sticky questions**

It might be a little
- personal.
- touchy.
- controversial.
- inappropriate.

If you don't want to answer . . .

B: No offense, but I feel a little uncomfortable talking about politics. I hope you don't mind.

A: Absolutely not. It's a good thing I asked.

B 🔊 5:07 **Rhythm and intonation** Listen again and repeat. Then practice the Conversation Model with a partner.

PRONUNCIATION | *Stress to emphasize meaning*

A 🔊 5:09 Listen to the different intonations of the same sentence. Then listen again and repeat.

1 Are you a conservative? (normal stress—no special meaning)

2 ARE you a conservative? (I think you're a conservative, but I'd like to be sure.)

3 Are **YOU** a conservative? (I'm surprised that you, among all people, would be a conservative.)

4 Are you a con**SERV**ative? (I'm surprised that you would have such a belief.)

B Pair work Practice varying the stress in this statement: "Would you say you're an independent?" Discuss the different meanings.

GRAMMAR — Non-count nouns that represent abstract ideas

GRAMMAR BOOSTER ▸ p. 136

- Count and non-count nouns: review and extension

Nouns that represent abstract ideas are always non-count nouns.

Education is an important issue.
NOT: ~~The~~ education is an important issue.
NOT: ~~Educations are~~ an important issue.

The news* about politics is always interesting.
NOT: The news about ~~the~~ politics is always interesting.
NOT: The news about politics ~~are~~ always interesting.

Abstract idea nouns

advice	patience
crime	peace
education	politics
health	poverty
help	progress
information	proof
investment	success
justice	time
news	work

*The word <u>news</u> is always singular. When it refers to a report in the press, on radio, TV, or the Internet, it is commonly referred to as <u>the news</u>.

A Grammar practice Complete each statement by choosing the correct form of the nouns and verbs.

1 Our (advice / advices) to you (is / are) to avoid discussing politics.

2 (Poverty / The poverty) (was / were) the topic of the international conference.

3 Both candidates have programs for (the health / health) and (educations / education).

4 Making (peace / the peace) takes a lot of (work / works) and a long time.

5 Good news (is / are) hard to find in the newspaper these days.

B Correct the errors.

Here's some political ~~informations~~ *information* about the election. The good news are that both candidates have programs for the education. The liberal candidate, Bill Slate, says financial helps for the schools are a question of the justice. The poverty has affected the quality of the schools, and students from schools in poor areas don't have a success. Joanna Clark, the conservative candidate, disagrees. She believes a progress has been made by investing in the teacher education. Her advices are to keep the old policy. "Creating better schools takes the time and a patience," she says.

NOW YOU CAN Bring up a controversial subject

A Which questions are too personal or controversial?

- ❏ What advice would you like to give the president / prime minister / king / queen?
- ❏ What do you think about the president / prime minister / king / queen?
- ❏ What should be done to decrease poverty?
- ❏ What would be necessary for peace in ___ ?
- ❏ What do you think about our ___ policy?
- ❏ Are you liberal or conservative?
- ❏ Who are you voting for in the election?

B Pair work Change the Conversation Model to bring up a topic that might be controversial. Partner B can decline to discuss the question. Then change roles.

A: Do you mind if I ask you a political question? I hope it's not too ....

B: No problem. What would you like to know?

A: Well, ... ?

B: Actually, ...

Don't stop!
Ask other questions that you don't think are too personal.

C Change partners Discuss another controversial subject.

GOAL **Discuss controversial issues politely**

CONVERSATION MODEL

A 🔊)) 5:10 Read and listen to a polite conversation about a controversial issue.

A: How do you feel about capital punishment?

B: I'm in favor of it. I believe if you kill someone you deserve to be killed. What about you?

A: Actually, I'm against the death penalty. I think it's wrong to take a life, no matter what.

B: Well, I guess we'll have to agree to disagree!

B 🔊)) 5:11 **Rhythm and intonation** Listen again and repeat. Then practice the Conversation Model with a partner.

C Discussion Are you in favor of capital punishment? Explain.

🔊)) 5:12 **Agreement**
I agree with you on that one.
I couldn't agree more.
I couldn't have said it better myself.
That's exactly what I think.

🔊)) 5:13 **Disagreement**
I guess we'll have to agree to disagree.
Really? I have to disagree with you there.
Do you think so? I'm not sure I agree.
Well, I'm afraid I don't agree.
No offense, but I just can't agree.

VOCABULARY *Some controversial issues*

A 🔊)) 5:14 Read and listen. Then listen again and repeat.

censorship of books and movies

compulsory military service

lowering the driving age

raising the voting age

prohibiting smoking indoors

B 🔊 5:15 **Listening comprehension** Listen to people's opinions about controversial issues. Complete the chart with the issue they discuss. Use the Vocabulary.

C 🔊 5:16 Now listen again and check <u>For</u> or <u>Against</u> in the chart, according to what the person says.

	Issue	For	Against
1			
2			
3			
4			
5			

GRAMMAR *Verbs followed by objects and infinitives*

GRAMMAR BOOSTER ▸ p. 137

- *Gerunds and infinitives: review*
  - *form and usage*
  - *usage after certain verbs*

Certain verbs can be followed by infinitives, but some verbs must be followed by an object before an infinitive.

The newspaper reminded **all 18-year-olds** <u>to vote</u>.
We urged **them** <u>to write</u> letters against the death penalty.

Verbs followed directly by an infinitive:

agree	decide	manage	pretend
appear	deserve	need	refuse
can't afford	hope	offer	seem
can't wait	learn	plan	

Verbs followed by an object before an infinitive:

advise	convince	permit	request	urge
allow	encourage	persuade	require	warn
cause	invite	remind	tell	

For a review of gerunds and infinitives, open **Reference Charts** on your *ActiveBook* Self-Study Disc.

A Grammar practice Complete each statement or question with an object and an infinitive.

1 The newspaper advised ....*all voters to register*.... early for the next election.
                         all voters / register

2 Did you remind .... her voter registration card?
                  your daughter / complete

3 We persuaded .... for our candidate.
               our friends / vote

4 Our teacher always encourages .... every night, not just the day before the exam.
                          students / study

5 Can't we convince .... on property?
             legislators / lower taxes

B On a separate sheet of paper, write two sentences using verbs that can be followed directly by an infinitive and two sentences with verbs that must have an object before an infinitive.

NOW YOU CAN **Discuss controversial issues politely**

Issues
- censorship
- compulsory military service for men and / or women
- lowering / raising the voting or driving age
- prohibiting smoking indoors
- Your own issue _____

A Pair work Use an issue from the list to change the Conversation Model. Use the Agreement and Disagreement Vocabulary from page 102. Then change roles and issues. Start like this:

A: How do you feel about .... ?

B: ....

Don't stop!
Ask your partner's opinion of other issues. Provide reasons to support your point of view.

♻ **Be sure to recycle this language.**

I'm against ___.
I'm in favor of ___.
I think / believe / feel:
  it's wrong.
  it's right.
  it's OK under some circumstances.
  it's wrong, no matter what.
  it depends.

B Change partners Discuss another issue, giving reasons to support your opinion.

BEFORE YOU READ

Explore your ideas What is the difference between a problem and a global problem? Do you think your generation faces more serious global problems than the generation of your parents or grandparents? Explain.

READING 5:17

The following issues were most frequently mentioned in a global survey about current world problems.

Corruption People all over the world complain about the corruption of police, government officials, and business leaders. Two examples of corruption are:

- A police officer takes money (a "bribe") from a driver so he doesn't give the driver a ticket for speeding.

- A company that wants to do business with a government agency offers a public official money or a gift to choose that company for the job.

Some people feel that power promotes corruption and that corruption is unavoidable. But an independent media—for example, non-government-backed newspapers, television stations, and Internet blogs—can also play an important role in exposing corruption.

Poverty Approximately one-fifth of the world's population, over 1 billion people, earns less than US $1.00 a day. Each day, over a billion people in the world lack basic food supplies. And according to UNICEF, each day, 25,000 children under the age of five die of starvation or preventable infectious disease.

There are many causes of poverty, ranging from catastrophic natural events to bad economic and agricultural policies, so there's no one solution to poverty worldwide. Some people feel that wealthy nations must send aid to poorer nations, while others are concerned that nothing will help unless local corruption is reduced and bad government policies are changed.

Terrorism Every day, we see or hear about suicide bombings and other violent acts committed against innocent people for religious or political reasons. Many ask why terrorism is on the rise.

Some social scientists believe that television and movies may contribute to growing anger. They claim that some people may feel frustrated and powerless when they measure their lives against the lives of extremely wealthy people they see in the media.

However, views about what causes terrorism can be very controversial, and many people disagree about its causes or possible solutions. While some feel that terrorism can be met with military force, others believe that people's extreme poverty and powerlessness must be reduced to make a difference.

Racism and discrimination Racism (the belief that one's own race or ethnic group is superior to others) and racial and ethnic discrimination (treating members of other groups unfairly) exist in many places. These two common problems cause human rights violations all over the world. In some cases a more powerful ethnic or racial group justifies the domination and, horribly, even the complete destruction of ethnic or racial minorities they consider to be inferior. When taken to this extreme, genocides such as the European Holocaust and the massacre in Sudan have threatened to wipe out entire peoples.

Can racism and discrimination be eliminated—or are these simply unfortunate features of human nature? Many people believe that education can help build tolerance of the "other" and may contribute to creating a more peaceful world.

A Activate language from a text Based on the information in the Reading, cross out the one word or phrase that is unrelated to the others. Explain your reasoning.

1	people	politics	ethnic groups	races
2	money	property	income	racism
3	bribe	corruption	discrimination	money
4	hunger	starvation	domination	lack of food
5	racism	business	discrimination	prejudice

B Understand from context Match each definition with a word from the box.

...... **1** a lack of necessary money to survive

...... **2** the attempt to destroy all members of a racial or ethnic group

...... **3** judging or harming people because of their racial or ethnic heritage

...... **4** money paid or some other reward given to a person to perform a dishonest or unethical act or to provide a favor

...... **5** the abuse of power by people in government or business

...... **6** the belief that other racial or ethnic groups are inferior to one's own

> **a** a bribe
> **b** genocide
> **c** poverty
> **d** corruption
> **e** discrimination
> **f** racism

C Critical thinking Discuss each of the following.

1 Reread the section on corruption in the Reading. What do all acts of corruption have in common? Do you think it is possible to end corruption, or do you feel that it is an "unavoidable part of human nature"? Use specific examples in your discussion.

2 What are some of the causes of poverty, and what are its effects? How is the problem of poverty related to all of the other problems mentioned in the Reading?

3 In your opinion, why do people engage in acts of terrorism? Is terrorism an expression of power or powerlessness and frustration? Provide examples to support your opinion.

4 What reasons do people have to hate other groups? Is hatred of another group ever understandable, appropriate, or justified? Explain the reasons for your opinion.

> On your *ActiveBook* Self-Study Disc:
> **Extra Reading Comprehension Questions**

NOW YOU CAN Propose solutions to global problems

A Frame your ideas On a scale of 1 to 6, put the ideas in order of importance and their difficulty to accomplish (1= most important or most difficult).

B Notepadding Write some possible solutions to global problems.

Problem	Possible solutions

Order of importance		Order of difficulty to accomplish
○	reducing poverty and hunger	○
○	preventing terrorism	○
○	avoiding war	○
○	ending or reducing corruption	○
○	wiping out racism and ethnic discrimination	○
○	protecting human rights	○

C Discussion Discuss the solutions to the global problems you proposed. Do you all have the same concerns?

Text-mining (optional)
Underline language in the Reading on page 104 to use in your discussion. For example: "There's no one solution to ___."

BEFORE YOU LISTEN

A 🔊 **Vocabulary** • *How to debate an issue politely* Read and listen. Then listen again and repeat.
5:18

1

❝I think smoking is a disgusting habit.❞

❝**That may be true, but** if you only smoke in your own house, you're not hurting anyone but yourself.❞

2

❝I think more people should be active in politics. That way, we would have better governments.❞

❝**I see what you mean, but** it's not realistic to expect everyone to care.❞

3

❝I think our president is doing an excellent job.❞

❝**Well, on the one hand,** he's not corrupt. **But on the other hand,** he hasn't done much to improve the country.❞

4

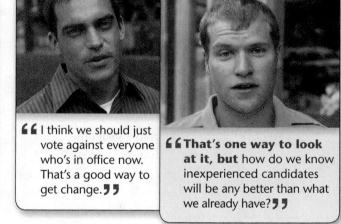

❝I think we should just vote against everyone who's in office now. That's a good way to get change.❞

❝**That's one way to look at it, but** how do we know inexperienced candidates will be any better than what we already have?❞

B **Pair work** Take turns saying and responding to each opinion. Use the Vocabulary above to disagree politely. Or, if you agree with the opinion, use the language of agreement from page 102. For example:

1 "In some countries, dictatorship has helped stop corruption."

❝I couldn't agree more. Countries with dictatorships are better off.❞ **OR** ❝That may be true, but no one should have to live under a dictatorship.❞

2 "There is no real democracy. All governments are controlled by a few powerful people."

3 "I think moderates are the only people you can trust in government."

4 "I'm not going to vote. All the candidates are corrupt."

5:19

🔊)) **Listen to summarize** Listen to three conversations about dictatorship, democracy, and monarchy. Then listen again, and on a separate sheet of paper, take notes about the arguments in favor of and against each system of government. Then, work in pairs. Partner A: Summarize the arguments in favor. Partner B: Summarize the arguments against.

NOW YOU CAN Debate the pros and cons of issues

A Group work Choose an issue that you'd like to debate.

- Banning text-messaging while driving
- Decriminalizing the use of illegal drugs
- Preventing children from going to movie theaters to see extremely violent movies
- Using the military to fight terrorism
- Permitting people to say or write anything as long as it doesn't cause physical danger
- Your own local or political issue:

  _____

B Notepadding On your notepad, write arguments in favor and against.

Issue:
Arguments in favor:
Arguments against:

C Debate Divide the group into two teams, with one team in favor and the other team against. Take turns presenting your views. Use the Vocabulary. Sit or stand with the people on your team. Take turns and disagree politely. Then continue the discussion.

♻️ **Be sure to recycle this language.**

Discuss controversies	Express agreement	Express disagreement
Are you in favor of ___ ?	I agree with you on that one.	We'll have to agree to disagree!
It's not cool to ___ .	I couldn't agree more.	I have to disagree with you there.
I tend to be a little opinionated.	I couldn't have said it better myself.	I'm not sure I agree.
I'm opposed to / in favor of ___ .	That's exactly what I think.	I'm afraid I don't agree.
I think / believe / feel:		No offense, but I can't agree.
it's wrong.		
it's right.		
it's OK under some circumstances.		
it's wrong, no matter what.		

Review

A 🔊 **Listening comprehension** Listen to the news report about four news
stories. Then listen again and complete each statement.

5:20

1 Sorindians and Ramays are two (ethnic groups / governments) that occupy land areas next to each other.

2 (Sorindians / Ramays) want to be able to observe their dietary laws and traditional clothing customs.

3 The problem between the Sorindians and the Ramays is an example of (corruption / ethnic discrimination).

4 A package left in the bathroom at the central post office raised fears of (terrorism / corruption).

5 Poor people are migrating into the (city from the countryside / countryside from the city).

6 Another story in the news is the reported (corruption / poverty) of a police captain.

B Complete the paragraph about an election, using verbs and count and non-count nouns correctly.

Many .... running for election make .... about ....
........1 candidate / candidates........ ....2 promise / promises........ ....3 education / the education........
But .... comes slowly, and .... hard to get.
........4 progress / the progress........ ....5 information / informations........ ....6 is / are........
Voters would like to see .... that their ....
........7 proof / proofs........ ....8 advice / advices........ ....9 is / are........
being followed. For instance, we are just now receiving .... of education statistics and
........10 news / the news........
.... not very good. .... is needed, and .... is necessary
........11 it's / they're........ ....12 Help / The help........ ....13 the time / time........
to improve our schools.

C Complete each sentence.

1 The law doesn't allow the president .... (change) the Constitution.

2 Our friends advised us .... (not / be) disappointed about the election.

3 The Constitution requires senators .... (leave) office after two terms.

4 The election committee permitted the candidates .... (speak) about their educational policies.

D Disagree politely with the following statements, using a different way
to disagree for each. Then add a reason why you disagree with each
statement.

That's one way to look at it, but . . .

1 Monarchies are dictatorships.

(YOU) ....

....

2 There's no such thing as a real democracy anywhere in the world.

(YOU) ....

....

5:21/5:22

🎵 **Top Notch Pop**
"We Can Agree to Disagree"
Lyrics p. 150

3 All people with power are corrupt.

(YOU) ....

....

E **Writing** On a separate sheet of paper, write at least two paragraphs about one
of the following issues: compulsory military service, capital punishment, or
censorship of books and movies. Include both the pros and cons of the issue.

WRITING BOOSTER ▸ p. 147

• *Contrasting ideas*
• *Guidance for Exercise E*

Contest Look at the pictures for one minute. Then close your books and name the three issues depicted in the news.

Pair work

1 Create a conversation between the man and woman in Picture 1. Continue the conversation, discussing corruption in general. Start like this:

Look at this article about the judge who was taking bribes in court.

2 Create a conversation between the two women in Picture 2. Start like this and continue the conversation, discussing terrorism in general:

A: Look! Another terrorist bombing.
B: Terrible! What do you think causes this?

3 Create a conversation between the two men discussing the election in Senegal in Picture 3. Start like this and continue the conversation:

I'm for Leon Mubumba. I'm a moderate. I think ...

CITY POST
Judge to prison for taking bribes.

Daily Gazette
Car bomb explodes near open-air market.
Numerous casualties. Unknown group claims responsibility.

ELECTION IN SENEGAL

NOW I CAN... ✓

- [ ] Bring up a controversial subject.
- [ ] Discuss controversial issues politely.
- [ ] Propose solutions to global problems.
- [ ] Debate the pros and cons of issues.

Beautiful World

GOALS After Unit 10, you will be able to:

1 Describe a geographical location.
2 Warn about a possible risk.
3 Describe a natural setting.
4 Discuss solutions to global warming.

The Arenal Volcano

CENTRAL AMERICA

COSTA RICA

Caribbean Sea

Lake Nicaragua

NICARAGUA

Lake Arenal

Arenal Volcano

Liberia

La Fortuna

COSTA RICA

9

7

Puntarenas

2

San José ★

▲ Irazu Volcano

Puerto Limón

Gulf of Nicoya

Quepos

5 4

3

Pacific Ocean

Coronado Bay

PANAMA

6

Gulf of Dulce

Mountain Ranges
1 Guanacaste Range
2 Central Volcanic Range
3 Talamanca Range
▲ = Volcano
● = City
★ = Capital City

National Parks
4 La Amistad
5 Chirripó
6 Corcovado
7 Braulio Carrillo
8 Santa Rosa
9 Tortuguero

0	50	100 kilometers
0	31	62 miles

The waterfall at La Fortuna

A 🔊 5:23 **Vocabulary** • *Geographical features* Read and listen. Then listen again and repeat.

a gulf	a lake	a sea	a mountain range
a bay	an ocean	a volcano	a national park

B Use the map to answer the questions about Costa Rica.

1 What two countries share a border with Costa Rica?

2 In what mountain range is Costa Rica's capital located?

3 What is Costa Rica's largest national park?

4 What is Costa Rica's largest lake?

5 Approximately how far is Puntarenas from San José?

6 What bodies of water are on Costa Rica's two coasts?

C 🔊 **Photo story** Read and listen to two tourists talking about Costa Rica.

Max: Have you folks been here long?

Frank: A little over a week. Unfortunately, we've only got two days left. You?

Max: We just got here yesterday, actually.

Frank: I'm Frank, by the way. Frank Lew. From Hong Kong.

Max: Max Belli. From Labro, Italy. Have you heard of it?

Frank: I can't say I have.

Max: It's a very small town about 20 kilometers north of Rome.

Max: Hey, you wouldn't happen to know anything about the La Fortuna waterfall, would you? We plan on driving up there this weekend.

Frank: Actually, we just got back from there yesterday.

Max: What a coincidence! Was it worth seeing?

Frank: Spectacular. You don't want to miss it.

Frank: But be sure to take it slow on the path down to the bottom of the falls. It can get pretty wet and slippery.

Max: Thanks for the warning. What if we want to get a look at the Arenal Volcano, too? Do you think that's doable in two days?

Frank: No problem. The volcano's only about twenty minutes west of La Fortuna by car. So I'm sure you could handle them both.

Max: Italian speaker / Frank: Chinese speaker

D Paraphrase Say each of the following statements from the Photo Story in your own way. Use the context of the story to help you restate each one.

1 "I can't say I have." ....

2 "What a coincidence!" ....

3 "Was it worth seeing?" ....

4 "You don't want to miss it." ....

5 ". . . be sure to take it slow." ....

6 "Do you think that's doable in two days?" ....

7 ". . . I'm sure you could handle them both." ....

E Pair work Brainstorm and write the names of places you know for each of the following geographical features.

an ocean or sea		a national park	
a bay or gulf		a lake	
a mountain or volcano		a waterfall	
a mountain range		a capital	

F Guessing game Describe a geographical feature of your country. Your classmates guess what place it is.

❝It's a beautiful lake. It's between . . .❞

❝It's a volcano. It's near . . .❞

GOAL Describe a geographical location

GRAMMAR *Prepositions of geographical place*

GRAMMAR BOOSTER ▸ p. 138

- Prepositions of place: more usage
- Proper nouns: capitalization
- Proper nouns: use of *the*

Look at the map and study the examples.

Mexico is north **of** (OR **to** the north **of**) Guatemala.
Honduras and El Salvador are located **to** the south.

Tikal is **in** the north. Guatemala City is **in** the south.
Cobán is located **in** the central part **of** Guatemala.

Champerico is **on** the west coast **of** Guatemala.
Flores is **on** the south shore **of** Lake Petén Itzá.
El Rancho is located **on** the Motagua River.

A Grammar practice Complete the sentences with the correct prepositions.

1 Vladivostok is located …….. the eastern coast …….. Russia.

2 Barranquilla is …….. the northern part …….. Colombia.

3 Haikou is …….. the northern coast …….. Hainan Island in China.

4 Machu Picchu is located about 100 kilometers northwest …….. Cuzco.

5 Vietnam is located south …….. China.

6 Kota Kinabalu is …….. the north coast of Borneo, a part of Malaysia.

7 Manaus is located …….. the Amazon River in Brazil.

8 Canada is …….. the north …….. the United States.

B Pair work On a separate sheet of paper, write and discuss the locations of five places in or near your country.

5:25
🔊)) **Directions**
N = north NE = northeast
S = south NW = northwest
E = east   SE = southeast
W = west   SW = southwest
Note: the **east** coast (OR **eastern** coast)

PRONUNCIATION *Voiced and voiceless* th

5:26
A 🔊)) Read and listen. Then listen again and repeat.

Voiced <u>th</u>	Voiceless <u>th</u>
1 the west	1 north
2 this way	2 northeastern
3 northern	3 south
4 southern	4 southwestern

B Pair work Take turns reading the sentences you wrote in Exercise B Pair Work above, paying attention to voiced and voiceless <u>th</u> sounds.

CONVERSATION MODEL

A 🔊 *5:27* Read and listen to someone describing a geographical location.

A: Where exactly is the temple located?

B: About fifteen kilometers north of Kyoto. Are you planning to go there?

A: I've been thinking about it.

B: It's a must-see. Be sure to take pictures!

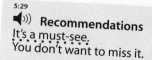

🔊 *5:29* **Recommendations**
It's a must-see.
You don't want to miss it.

🔊 *5:30* **Criticisms**
It's overrated.
It's a waste of time.

B 🔊 *5:28* **Rhythm and intonation** Listen again and repeat. Then practice the Conversation Model with a partner.

NOW YOU CAN   Describe a geographical location

A Pair work Change the Conversation Model to talk about the location of an interesting place. Use the map and the pictures or a map of your own country. Then change roles.

A: Where exactly is .... located?

B: .... Are you planning to go there?

A: I've been thinking about it.

B: ....

Don't stop!
• Ask more questions about the place.
  Is it worth seeing?
  Is it doable in [one day]?
• Ask about other places.

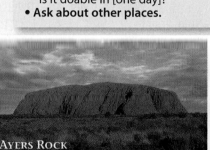
AYERS ROCK

THE GREAT BARRIER REEF

KAKADU NATIONAL PARK

THE SNOWY MOUNTAINS

B Change partners Describe other places.

GOAL **Warn about a possible risk**

VOCABULARY *Describe possible risks*

A 🔊 5:31 Read and listen. Then listen again and repeat.

It can be quite **dangerous**.

It can be very **rocky**.

It can be extremely **steep**.

It can be so **slippery**.

It can be pretty **dark**.

It can be terribly **exhausting**.

It can be really **foggy**.

🔊 5:32 **Some places**

a path
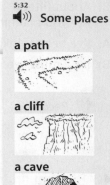

a cliff

a cave

🔊 5:33 **Dangerous animals and insects**
Watch out for [snakes].
Keep an eye out for [bears].

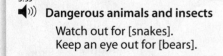

a snake   a shark

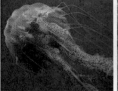

a jellyfish   a bear

a scorpion   a mosquito

B 🔊 5:34 **Listening comprehension** Listen to the conversations.
Check if the speaker thinks the place is safe or dangerous.

	Safe	Dangerous
1 He thinks hiking around the waterfall is . . .	☐	☐
2 She thinks climbing the mountain is . . .	☐	☐
3 She thinks swimming in the bay is . . .	☐	☐
4 He thinks walking on the cliffs is . . .	☐	☐

C 🔊 5:35 Listen again. Complete each statement with the dangers.

1 He warns that the path is .... and there may be
....

2 She warns that there may be .... and that the path
can be ....

3 He's worried that there will be a lot of .... and there
may be ....

4 He warns that the cliffs are .... and there may be
....

GRAMMAR _Too_ + adjective and infinitive

Use _too_ + an adjective and an infinitive to give a warning or an explanation.
It's **too dark to go** hiking now. = You'd better not go hiking now because it's dark.
Those cliffs are **too steep to climb**. = You'd better not climb those cliffs because they're very steep.

Use a _for_ phrase to further clarify a warning or explanation.
It's too dangerous **for children** to go swimming there.
(Only adults should swim there.)

Be careful!
DON'T SAY: Those cliffs are too steep to climb ~~them~~.

Grammar practice Complete the sentences, using _too_ + an adjective and an infinitive with a _for_ phrase.

1 It's .... to that neighborhood alone.
   dangerous / you / go
2 The pyramid at Teotihuacán is ....
   steep / older tourists / climb
3 It's .... the last train to the capital.
   late / your friends / catch
4 The path is .... safely.
   rocky / your children / walk on
5 It's really .... hiking to the waterfall today.
   hot / us / go
6 Don't you think this map is .... ?
   confusing / them / understand

CONVERSATION MODEL

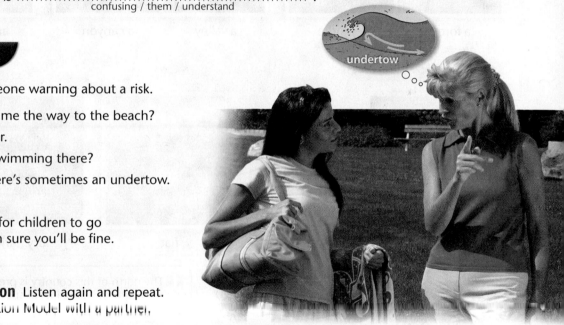

undertow

A 🔊 5:36 Read and listen to someone warning about a risk.

A: Excuse me. Can you tell me the way to the beach?

B: That way. It's not very far.

A: Thanks. Is it safe to go swimming there?

B: Sure, but be careful. There's sometimes an undertow.

A: Really?

B: Well, it's too dangerous for children to go swimming there. But I'm sure you'll be fine.

A: Thanks for the warning.

B 🔊 5:37 **Rhythm and intonation** Listen again and repeat. Then practice the Conversation Model with a partner.

NOW YOU CAN Warn about a possible risk

A Pair work Change the Conversation Model. Ask for directions to another place. Warn about possible risks. Then change roles.

A: Excuse me. Can you tell me the way to .... ?

B: ....

A: Thanks. Is it safe to .... there?

B: ....

B Change partners Warn about another place.

Places to go	Things to do
a waterfall	swim
a path	hike
a cave	walk
a beach	climb
cliffs	bike
	ski

Don't stop!
• **Ask for more information.**
   Do I need to watch out for snakes?
   Are there a lot of mosquitoes?
   Is the path very [steep]?
   Is it worth [seeing]?
• **Warn about other dangers.**
   Watch out for [jellyfish].
   It's too ___ [for ___] to ___ .

BEFORE YOU LISTEN

A 5:38 🔊 **Vocabulary** • *Describing the natural world* Read and listen.
Then listen again and repeat.

5:39
🔊 **Strong positive adjectives**
The scenery was **breathtaking**.
The views were **spectacular**.
The sights were **extraordinary**.

Geographic nouns

a forest

a jungle

a valley

a canyon

an island

a glacier

Geographic adjectives

mountainous

hilly

flat

dry / arid

lush / green

B **Pair work** Talk about places you know, using the nouns and adjectives from the Vocabulary.

❝ The north of this country is pretty arid, but in the south there are lots of spectacular forests. ❞

LISTENING COMPREHENSION

A 5:40 🔊 **Listen for main ideas** Read the questions and listen to Kenji Ozaki describe a memorable trip he once took. Then answer the questions.

1 What country did Mr. Ozaki visit?

2 What kind of a place did he visit?

3 What do you think he liked best about it?

4 What geographical adjective best describes the place?

B 🔊 **Listen for details** Listen again to how Mr. Ozaki describes the natural features he saw on his trip. Complete each phrase with a word from the box.

1 beautiful ....

2 super-high ....

3 spectacular ....

4 an ancient ....

5 extraordinary ....

6 breathtaking ....

7 fresh ....

8 natural ....

forest	air
waterfalls	beauty
canyon	water
mountains	cliffs
views	trees

C **Summarize** In your own words, describe Mr. Ozaki's trip by restating key details. Listen again if necessary.

NOW YOU CAN   Describe a natural setting

A **Frame your ideas** Choose a photo. Describe the place and what a person could do there. Your partner guesses which place you chose.

" It's a lush island in a beautiful ocean. You can lie on the beach and do nothing or go snorkeling. "

Tahiti

The Galapagos Islands, Ecuador

Tibet

Alaska

Iguazu Falls, Brazil and Argentina

B **Notepadding** On your notepad, write about a spectacular place you know or a place you'd like to visit. What does it look like? What can you do there?

Name of place:	Things you can do there:
Description:	

C **Pair work** Tell your partner about the place you wrote about on your notepad. Use the Vocabulary.

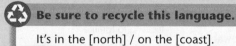 **Be sure to recycle this language.**

It's in the [north] / on the [coast].
It's located on the [Orinoco River] / the east coast / shore of [Lake Victoria].
It's south of ___.
It's in the central part of ___.
It's a must-see.

You don't want to miss it.
[Bash Bish Falls] is overrated, but [Niagara Falls] is breathtaking.
[Saw Valley] is a waste of time, but [Pine Valley] is extraordinary.
It's very rocky / steep / slippery.

117

BEFORE YOU READ

A 5:42 **Vocabulary • *Ways to talk about the environment*** Read and listen. Then listen again and repeat.

the environment *n.* the air, water, and land in which people, animals, and plants live

pollution *n.* the act of causing air, water, or land to become dirty and unhealthy for people, plants, and animals

power *n.* electricity or other force that can be used to make machines, cars, etc., work

renewable energy *n.* power for heat and machines, such as wind power or solar power from the sun, that can be reused and never run out

energy-efficient *adj.* uses as little power as possible

increase *v.* to become larger in amount
an increase in [temperature] *n.*

decrease *v.* to become smaller in amount
a decrease in [pollution] *n.*

B **Discussion** What do you already know about global warming? What causes it? What effect is it having on the environment?

READING   5:43

Choose Clean Energy and Help Curb Global Warming

Fossil fuels such as oil, coal, and natural gas—provide energy for our cars and homes, but increase the amount of carbon dioxide (CO_2) in the air, contributing to global warming. However, there are choices we can make that can lessen their negative impact on the environment.

Get Moving—Take good care of your car and keep your tires properly inflated with air. You will use less gasoline and save money. Better yet, skip the drive and walk, take public transportation, or ride a bicycle when you can.

Upgrade—Replace your old refrigerator or air-conditioner with a new energy-efficient model. Not only will you save money on your electric bill, but you'll contribute to cutting back on the pollution that causes global warming.

See the light—Use new energy-saving compact fluorescent light bulbs. They produce the same amount of light as older incandescent bulbs, but they use 25% less electricity and last much longer.

Cut back—Try to reduce the amount of water you use for showers, laundry, and washing dishes. And turn the temperature on your hot water heater down.

Recycle—Use products that are recycled from old paper, glass, and metal to reduce energy waste and pollution by 70 to 90%. And before you toss things in the garbage, think about what you can reuse.

Think local—Shipping foods over long distances is a waste of energy and adds to pollution. In addition, the pesticides and chemicals used to grow them are bad for the environment. So buy locally grown fruits and vegetables instead.

Speak out—Talk to lawmakers about your interest in curbing global warming. Support their attempts to improve standards for fuel efficiency, to fund renewable and clean energy solutions, such as wind and solar power, and to protect forests.

Information source: www.sierraclub.org

Compact flourescent light bulbs use less electricity.

The expected effects of global warming

- An increase in floods, droughts, tornadoes, and other extreme weather conditions
- A rise in sea levels, causing flooding in coastal areas
- Higher sea surface temperatures, endangering sea life
- The shrinking of glaciers, leading to a decrease in fresh water for rivers and less energy production
- A loss of tropical forests, an increase in arid lands, more forest fires, and a loss of animal and plant species
- A decrease in agricultural yields, leading to famine

Clean energy solutions like wind power can help curb global warming.

A Understand from context Find each of the following words or phrases in the Reading. Then use your understanding of the words to write definitions.

1 curb ....

2 fossil fuels ....

3 a negative impact ....

4 inflated ....

5 reduce ....

6 rise ....

B Critical thinking Discuss the following questions.

1 The article mentions fossil fuels as a major source of energy. What two other sources of energy are mentioned? How are they different from fossil fuels?

2 Look at the list of the effects of global warming in the Reading. What impact could they have on these aspects of your country's economy: tourism, food production, housing, and disaster relief?

C Summarize Review the article again. Then close your book. With a partner, discuss and make a list of the ways the article suggests you can help curb global warming.

On your *ActiveBook* Self-Study Disc:
Extra Reading Comprehension Questions

NOW YOU CAN   Discuss solutions to global warming

A Notepadding What do you do in your daily life that might contribute to the energy waste and pollution that causes global warming? Make a list on your notepad.

at home:
at work:
at school:
transportation:
other:

B Pair work Compare notepads with a partner. Discuss what you think each of you could do to help cut down on energy waste and pollution.

   ❝ I don't really recycle right now, but I'd like to. I think it would be better for the environment if I did. ❞

     ❝ I want to buy energy-efficient light bulbs, but they're so much more expensive than the regular kind. ❞

C Discussion Do you agree with the suggestions in the article? Discuss the value of trying to take personal actions to help curb global warming. Talk about:

- what you are doing now.
- what you'd like to do in the future.
- what you think is not worth doing.

♻ **Be sure to recycle this language.**

Are you in favor of ___ ?
I think / don't think it's a good idea to ___ .
I'm against ___ .
That's true, but ___ .
I see what you mean, but ___ .
On the one hand, ___ . But on the other hand, ___ .
That's one way to look at it, but ___ .
That depends.
We'll have to agree to disagree.

Text mining. (Optional)
Underline language in the Reading on page 118 to use in your discussion.
For example:
"___ is a waste of energy ..."

Review

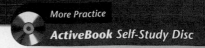
More Practice
ActiveBook *Self-Study Disc*
grammar · vocabulary · listening
reading · speaking · pronunciation

A 🔊 5:44 **Listening comprehension** Listen to the conversations and, using the word box, write the type of place each person is talking about. Then check whether or not the person recommends going there.

a canyon	cliffs	a glacier	a volcano
a cave	a desert	a valley	a waterfall

Type of place	Recommended?		Type of place	Recommended?
1	☐ yes ☐ no	**3**	....	☐ yes ☐ no
2	☐ yes ☐ no	**4**	....	☐ yes ☐ no

B Look at the pictures. Complete the warnings about each danger, using <u>too</u>.

1	**2**	**3**	**4**

1 That road .... to ride on if you're not careful.

2 Those steps .... climb safely after a rain.

3 .... go in the cave without a flashlight.

4 .... go swimming in the bay.

🎵 5:45/5:46
Top Notch Pop
"It's a Beautiful World"
Lyrics p. 150

C Complete the locations, using the map.

1 The town of Saint-Pierre .... an island.

2 Grand Barachois Bay .... the village of Miquelon.

3 The island of Saint-Pierre .... Langlade.

4 The village of Miquelon .... about .... from the town of Saint-Pierre.

5 The beaches .... the .... coast.

D Writing On a separate sheet of paper, write a description of your country, state, or province. Include the location and description of major cities, geographical features, national parks, and other points of interest. Use adjectives to provide details that help the reader see and feel what the places are like.

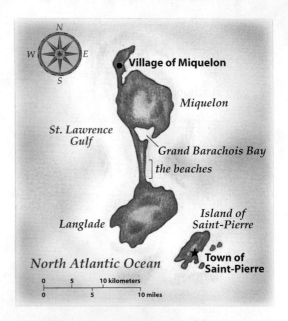

quiet / noisy	humid / dry	spectacular
crowded	flat	breathtaking
hot / warm	hilly	beautiful
cold / cool	mountainous	gorgeous

WRITING BOOSTER ▸ p. 148

- *Organizing by spatial relations*
- *Guidance for Exercise D*

Game Using the map and the pictures, describe a location or natural features. Your classmates guess the place. For example:

It's located south of Denali National Park. OR *It has spectacular glaciers.*

Pair work Use the map and the "Explore Alaska!" chart to create conversations for the man and the woman. Start like this:

Where exactly is __? OR *Excuse me. Could you tell me the way to __?*

Glacier Bay National Park

Katmai National Park

Arctic Ocean

N W E S

Alaska

Fairbanks

Denali National Park

Anchorage

Katmai National Park

CANADA

Juneau

Bering Sea

Kodiak Island

Glacier Bay National Park

0   500 miles

0   300 kilometers

Gulf of Alaska

Explore Alaska!

	bears	mosquitos	snakes	fog
Denali National Park	✓	✓	✗	✓
Kodiak Island	✓	✓	✗	✓
Katmai National Park	✓	✓	✗	✗
Glacier Bay National Park	✗	✗	✗	✓

NOW I CAN... ✔

- ☐ Describe a geographical location.
- ☐ Warn about a possible risk.
- ☐ Describe a natural setting.
- ☐ Discuss solutions to global warming.

Grammar Booster

The Grammar Booster is optional. It is not required for the achievement tests in the *Top Notch Complete Assessment Package.* If you use the Grammar Booster, there are extra Grammar Booster exercises in the Workbook in a separate labeled section.

UNIT 1 *Lesson 1*

Tag questions: short answers

Look at the affirmative and negative short answers to the tag questions from page 4.

You're Lee, **aren't you?**	Yes, I am. / No, I'm not.
You're not Amy, **are you?**	Yes, I am. / No, I'm not.
She speaks Thai, **doesn't she?**	Yes, she does. / No, she doesn't.
I don't know you, **do I?**	Yes, you do. / No, you don't.
He's going to drive, **isn't he?**	Yes, he is. / No, he isn't.
We're not going to eat here, **are we?**	Yes, we are. / No, we aren't.
They'll be here later, **won't they?**	Yes, they will. / No, they won't.
It won't be long, **will it?**	Yes, it will. / No, it won't.
You were there, **weren't you?**	Yes, I was. / No, I wasn't.
He wasn't driving, **was he?**	Yes, he was. / No, he wasn't.
They left, **didn't they?**	Yes, they did. / No, they didn't.
We didn't know, **did we?**	Yes, you did. / No, you didn't.
It's been a great day, **hasn't it?**	Yes it has. / No, it hasn't.
She hasn't been here long, **has she?**	Yes, she has. / No she hasn't.
Ann would like Quito, **wouldn't she?**	Yes, she would. / No, she wouldn't.
You wouldn't do that, **would you?**	Yes, I would. / No, I wouldn't.
They can hear me, **can't they?**	Yes, they can. / No, they can't.
He can't speak Japanese, **can he?**	Yes, he can. / No, he can't.

A **Complete each conversation by circling the correct tag question and completing the short answer.**

1 A: Mary would like to study foreign cultures (would / wouldn't) **she?**

   B: Yes, _____.

2 A: It's a long time until dinner, (is / isn't) **it?**

   B: No, _____.

3 A: We met last summer, (did / didn't) **we?**

   B: Yes, _____.

4 A: They're starting the meeting really late, (haven't / aren't) **they?**

   B: No, _____.

5 A: There weren't too many delays in the meeting, (wasn't it / were there)?

   B: No, _____.

6 A: You don't know what to do, (do / don't) **you?**

   B: No, _____.

7 A: There isn't any reason to call, (is / isn't) **there?**

   B: No, _____.

8 A: It's awful to not have time for lunch, (isn't it / aren't you)?

   B: Yes, _____.

9 A: When you know etiquette, you can feel comfortable anywhere, (can / can't) **you?**

   B: Yes, _____.

10 A: It's really getting late, (is it / isn't it)?

   B: No, _____.

B **Correct the error in each item.**

1 They'd both like to study abroad, ~~would~~ ^{wouldn't} they?

2 It's only a six-month course, is it?

3 Clark met his wife on a rafting trip, didn't Clark?

4 Marian made three trips to Japan last year, hasn't she?

5 There were a lot of English-speaking people on the tour, wasn't it?

6 The students don't know anything about that, don't they?

7 There isn't any problem with my student visa, isn't there?

8 It's always interesting to travel with people from other countries, aren't they?

9 With English, you can travel to most parts of the world, can you?

10 I'm next, don't I?

Verb usage: present and past (review)

Stative (non-action) verbs

appear	notice
be	own
believe	possess
belong	preter
contain	remember
cost	see
feel	seem
hate	smell
have	sound
hear	suppose
know	taste
like	think
look	understand
love	want
need	weigh

The simple present tense (but NOT the present continuous):
- **for facts and regular occurrences**
  I **study** English. Class **meets** every day. Water **boils** at 100°.
- **with frequency adverbs and time expressions**
  They never **eat** before 6:00 on weekdays.
- **with stative ("non-action") verbs**
  I **remember** her now.
- **for future actions, especially those indicating schedules**
  Flight 100 usually leaves at 2:00, but tomorrow it **leaves** at 1:30.

The present continuous (but NOT the simple present tense):
- **for actions happening now (but NOT with stative [non-action] verbs)**
  They**'re talking** on the phone.
- **for actions occurring during a time period in the present**
  This year I**'m studying** English.
- **for some future actions, especially those already planned**
  Thursday I**'m going** to the theater.

The present perfect or the present perfect continuous:
- **for unfinished or continuous actions**
  I**'ve lived** here since 2007. OR I**'ve been living** here since 2007.
  I**'ve lived** here for five years. OR I**'ve been living** here for five years.

The present perfect (but NOT the present perfect continuous):
- **for completed or non-continuing actions**
  I**'ve eaten** there three times.
  I**'ve never** read that book.
  I**'ve already seen** him.

The simple past tense:
- **for actions completed at a specified time in the past**
  I **ate** there in 2010. NOT I've eaten there in 2010.

The past continuous:
- **for one or more actions in progress at a time in the past**
  At 7:00, we **were eating** dinner.
  They **were swimming** and we **were sitting** on the beach.

The past continuous and the simple past tense:
- **for an action that interrupted a continuing action in the past**
  I **was eating** when my sister called.

Use to / used to :
- **for past situations and habits that no longer exist**
  I **used to smoke**, but I stopped.
  They **didn't use to require** a visa, but now they do.

The past perfect:
- **to indicate that one past action preceded another past action**
  When I arrived, they **had finished** lunch.

A Correct the verbs in the following sentences.

1 I talk on the phone with my fiancé right now.

2 She's usually avoiding sweets.

3 They eat dinner now and can't talk on the phone.

4 Every Friday I'm going to the gym at 7:00.

5 Burt is wanting to go home early.

6 Today we all study in the library.

7 The train is never leaving before 8:00.

8 Water is freezing when the temperature goes down.

9 We're liking coffee.

10 On most days I'm staying home.

B Complete each sentence with the present perfect continuous.

1 We _____ to this spa for two years.
  come

2 *Slumdog Millionaire* _____ at the Classic Cinema since last Saturday.
  play

3 Robert _____ for an admissions letter from the language school for a week.
  wait

4 The tour operators _____ weather conditions for the rafting trip.
  worry about

5 I _____ that tour with everyone.
  talk about

C Check the sentences and questions that express unfinished or continuing actions. Then, on a separate sheet of paper, change the verb phrase in those sentences to the present perfect continuous.

The Averys have lived in New York since the late nineties.

The Averys have been living in New York since the late nineties.

☐ **1** Their relatives have already called them.

☐ **2** We have waited to see them for six months.

☐ **3** I haven't seen the Berlin Philharmonic yet.

☐ **4** This is the first time I've visited Dubai.

☐ **5** We have eaten in that old Peruvian restaurant for years.

☐ **6** Has he ever met your father?

☐ **7** How long have they studied Arabic?

☐ **8** My husband still hasn't bought a car.

☐ **9** The kids have just come back from the soccer game.

UNIT 2 *Lesson 1*

Other ways to draw conclusions: _probably_; _most likely_

Two other ways to draw conclusions are with **probably** and **most likely**. These indicate less certainty than **must**.

Probably frequently occurs after the verb **be**
or when **be** is part of a verb phrase.
  They're **probably** at the dentist's office.
  It's **probably** going to rain.

Use **probably** before **isn't** or **aren't**. With **is not**
or **are not**, use **probably** before **not**.
  She **probably** isn't feeling well.
  She's **probably** not feeling well.

Be careful! Don't use **probably** after verbs other than **be**.
Don't say: He ~~forgot probably~~ about the appointment.

Use **probably** before other verbs.
  He **probably** forgot about the appointment.
  The dentist **probably** doesn't have time to see a new patient.

You can also use **Probably** or **Most likely** at the beginning of a sentence to draw a conclusion.
  Probably she's a teacher. / **Most likely** she's a teacher.
  Probably he forgot about the appointment. / **Most likely** he forgot about the appointment.

On a separate sheet of paper, rewrite each sentence with **probably** or **most likely**.

1 He must have a terrible cold.

2 She must be feeling very nauseous.

3 They must not like going to the dentist.

4 The dentist must not be in her office today.

5 Acupuncture must be very popular in Asia.

6 A conventional doctor must have to study for a long time.

Expressing possibility with *maybe*

Maybe most frequently occurs at the beginning of a sentence.
Maybe he needs an X-ray. (= He may need an X-ray.)

Be careful! Don't confuse **maybe** and **may be**.
She **may be** a doctor.
NOT She ~~maybe~~ a doctor.
Maybe she's a doctor.
NOT ~~May be~~ she's a doctor.

On a separate sheet of paper, rewrite each sentence with _maybe_.

1 His doctor may use herbal therapy.

2 Conventional medicine may be the best choice.

3 The doctor may want to take a blood test.

4 She may prefer to wait until tomorrow.

5 They may be afraid to see a dentist.

UNIT 3 Lesson 1

Let to indicate permission

Use an object and the base form of a verb with **let**.

     object   base form
She **let her sister wear** her favorite skirt.

Be careful!
Don't say: She let her sister ~~to wear~~ her favorite skirt.

Let has the same meaning as **permit**.
Use **let** to indicate that permission is being given to do something.
My boss **let** me **take** the day off.
I **don't let** my children **stay** out after 9:00 P.M.
Why **don't** you **let** me **help** you?

A On a separate sheet of paper, rewrite each sentence, using _let_.

1 Don't permit your younger brother to open the oven door.

2 You should permit your little sister to go to the store with you.

3 We don't permit our daughter to eat a lot of candy.

4 I wouldn't permit my youngest son to go to the mall alone.

5 Why don't you permit your children to see that movie?

6 You should permit them to make their own decision.

7 We always permit him to stay out late.

Causative *have*: common errors

Be careful! Don't confuse the simple past tense causative _have_ with the past perfect auxiliary _have_.
I **had them call** me before 10:00   (They called me.)
I **had called** them before 10:00.   (I called them.)

B Who did what? Read each sentence. Complete each statement. Follow the example.

We had them fix the car before our trip.   _They_ fixed _the car_.
We had fixed the car before our trip.   _We_ fixed _the car_.

1 Janet had already called her mother.   _____ called _____.
  Janet had her mother call the train station.   _____ called _____.

2 Mark had his friends help him with moving.   _____ helped _____.
  Mark had helped his friends with moving.   _____ helped _____.

3 My father had signed the check for his boss. _____ signed _____.
  My father had his boss sign the check.   _____ signed _____.

4 Mr. Gates had them open the bank early.   _____ opened _____.
  Mr. Gates had opened the bank early.   _____ opened _____.

The passive causative: the <u>by</u> phrase

Use a <u>by</u> phrase if knowing who performed the action is important.
I had my dress shortened **by the tailor** at the shop next to the train station.

If knowing who performed the action is not important, you don't need to include a <u>by</u> phrase.
I had my dress shortened ~~by someone~~ at the shop next to the train station.

On a separate sheet of paper, use the cues to write advice about services, using <u>you should</u> and the passive causative <u>get</u> or <u>have</u>. Use a <u>by</u> phrase if the information is important. Follow the example.

shoe / repair / Mr. B / at the Boot Stop
You should get your shoes repaired by Mr. B at the Boot Stop.

1 picture / frame / Lydia / at Austin Custom Framing

2 hair / cut / Eva / at the Curl Up Hair Salon

3 photos / print / at the mall

4 a suit / make / Luigi / at Top Notch Tailors

5 sweaters / dry-clean / at Midtown Dry Cleaners

Verbs that can be followed by clauses with <u>that</u>

The following verbs often have noun clauses as their direct objects. Notice that each verb expresses a kind of "mental activity." In each case, it is optional to include <u>that</u>.

She	agrees thinks believes feels	(that) the students should work harder.	I	assume suppose doubt guess	(that) they made reservations.
We	hear see understand hope	(that) the government has a new plan.	He	forgot noticed realized remembered knew	(that) the stores weren't open.
They	decided discovered dreamed hoped learned	(that) everyone could pass the test.			

Adjectives that can be followed by clauses with <u>that</u>

Use a clause with <u>that</u> after a predicate adjective of emotion to further explain its meaning.

I'm	afraid angry	(that) we'll have to leave early.	He's	sorry unhappy	(that) the flight was cancelled.
We're	worried ashamed	(that) we won't be on time to the event.	She's	surprised disappointed	(that) the news spread so fast.
They're	happy sad	(that) the teacher is leaving.			

On a separate sheet of paper, complete each sentence in your own way. Use clauses with <u>that</u>.

1 When I was young, I couldn't believe . . .
2 Last year, I decided . . .
3 This year, I was surprised to discover . . .
4 Last week, I forgot . . .
5 Recently, I heard . . .
6 In the future, I hope . . .

7 Now that I study English, I know . . .
8 In the last year, I learned . . .
9 Not long ago, I remembered . . .
10 Recently, I dreamed . . .
11 (your own idea)
12 (your own idea)

UNIT 4 Lesson 2

Embedded questions: usage and common errors

You can use an embedded question to ask for information more politely.
Are we late? → Can you tell me **if we're late**?
What time is it? → Can you tell me **what time it is**?
Why isn't it working? → Could you explain **why it isn't working**?
Where's the bathroom? → Do you know **where the bathroom is**?
How do I get to the bank? → Would you mind telling me **how I get to the bank**?

Be careful! Do not use the question form in embedded questions.
Do you know **why she won't read** the newspaper?
Don't say: Do you know why ~~won't she~~ read the newspaper?

Can you tell me **if this bus runs** express?
Don't say: Can you tell me ~~does this bus run~~ express?

Phrases that are often followed by embedded questions
I don't know . . .
I'd like to know . . .
Let me know . . .
I can't remember . . .
Let's ask . . .
I wonder . . .
I'm not sure . . .

Do you know . . . ?
Can you tell me . . . ?
Can you remember . . . ?
Could you explain . . . ?
Would you mind telling me . . . ?

Embedded questions: punctuation

Sentences with embedded questions are punctuated according to the meaning of the whole sentence.

If an embedded question is in a sentence, use a period.
I don't know (something). → I don't know **who she is.**

If an embedded question is in a question, use a question mark.
Can you tell me (something)? → Can you tell me **who she is?**

A On a separate sheet of paper, complete each sentence with an embedded question. Punctuate each sentence correctly.

1 Please let me know (When does the movie start?)
2 I wonder (Where is the subway station?)
3 Can you tell me (How do you know that?)
4 We're not sure (What should we bring for dinner?)
5 They'd like to understand (Why doesn't Pat want to come to the meeting?)
6 Please tell the class (Who painted this picture?)

B On a separate sheet of paper, rewrite each question more politely, using noun clauses with embedded questions. Begin each one with a different phrase. Follow the example.

Where's the airport? *Can you tell me where the airport is?*

1 What time does the concert start?
2 How does this new MP3 player work?
3 Why is the express train late?
4 Where is the nearest bathroom?
5 Who speaks English at that hotel?
6 When does Flight 18 arrive from Paris?

C Correct the wording and punctuation errors in each item.

1 Could you please tell me does this train go to Nagoya.

2 I was wondering can I get your phone number?

3 I'd like to know what time does the next bus arrive?

4 Can you tell me how much does this magazine cost.

5 Do you remember where did he use to live?

6 I'm not sure why do they keep calling me.

7 I wonder will she come on time?

Embedded questions with infinitives

In embedded questions, an infinitive can be used to express possibility (<u>can</u> or <u>could</u>) or advice (<u>should</u>).
You can use an infinitive after the question word. The following sentences have the same meaning.

I don't know **where I can get** that magazine. = I don't know **where to get** that magazine.

I'm not sure **when I should call** them. = I'm not sure **when to call** them.

She wanted to know **which train she should take**. = She wanted to know **which train to take**.

You can also use an infinitive after <u>whether</u>.

I can't decide **whether I should read** this book next. = I can't decide **whether to read** this book next.

Be careful! Don't use an infinitive after <u>if</u>. Use <u>whether</u> instead.

I can't decide **if I should read** this book next. = I can't decide **whether to read** this book next.

Don't say: I can't decide ~~if to read~~ this book next.

D On a separate sheet of paper, rewrite each sentence with an infinitive.

1 Could you tell me whose novel I should read next?

2 I'd like to know where I can buy Smith's latest book.

3 Can you remember who I should call to get that information?

4 I'd like to know which train I can take there.

5 Let me know if I should give her the magazine when I'm done.

6 I wasn't sure when I could get the new edition of her book.

7 Let's ask how we can get to the train station.

Noun clauses as subjects and objects

A noun clause can function as either a subject or an object in a sentence.

As a subject	As an object
What he wrote inspired many people.	I like **what he wrote**.
Where the story takes place is fascinating.	I want to know **where the story takes place**.
How she became a writer is an interesting story.	They are inspired by **how she became a writer**.
That she wrote the novel in six months is amazing.	I heard **that she wrote the novel in six months**.
Who wrote the article isn't clear.	I wonder **who wrote the article**.

E On a separate sheet of paper, use the prompts to write sentences with noun clauses.

1 People always ask me (Why did I decide to study English?)

2 (She wrote science fiction novels.) has always fascinated me.

3 We all wanted to know (Where did she go on vacation?)

4 (What websites do you visit?) is important information for companies who want to sell you their products.

5 Can you tell me (Who did you invite to dinner?)

6 (How did you decide to become a teacher?) is an interesting story.

Direct speech: punctuation rules

When writing direct speech, use quotation marks to indicate the words the speaker actually said.
Put final punctuation marks before the second quotation mark.
Jeremy said, "Don't answer the phone."

Use a comma after the verb or verb phrase that introduces the quoted speech.
They said, "Call me after the storm."

Begin the quoted speech with a capital letter.
I said, "Please come to dinner at nine."

A On a separate sheet of paper, write and punctuate each of the following statements in direct speech. Follow the example.

They said tell us when you will be home

They said, "Tell us when you will be home."

1 Martin told me don't get a flu shot

2 My daughter said please pick me up after school

3 The English teacher said read the newspaper tonight and bring in a story about the weather

4 We said please don't forget to listen to the news

5 They said don't buy milk

6 We told them please call us in the morning

7 She said please tell your parents I'm sorry I can't talk right now

B Look at each statement in indirect speech. Then on a separate sheet of paper, complete each statement. Using the prompt, make the indirect speech statement a direct speech statement. Use correct punctuation.

1 They told us to be home before midnight. (They told us)

2 The sign downtown said to pack emergency supplies before the storm. (The sign downtown said)

3 Your daughter called and told me to turn on the radio and listen to the news about the flood. (Your daughter told me)

4 Your parents said not to call them before 9 A.M. (Your parents said)

5 Mr. Rossi phoned to tell me not to go downtown this afternoon. (Mr. Rossi phoned to tell me)

Indirect speech: optional tense changes

When the reporting verbs <u>say</u> or <u>tell</u> are in the simple past tense, it is not always necessary to use a different tense in indirect speech from the one the speaker used. The following are three times when it's optional:

When the statement refers to something JUST said:
I just heard the news. They said a storm **is** coming.
OR I just heard the news. They said a storm **was** coming.

When the quoted speech refers to something that's still true:
May told us she **wants** to get a flu shot tomorrow.
OR May told us she **wanted** to get a flu shot tomorrow.

When the quoted speech refers to a scientific or general truth:
They said that English **is** an international language.
OR They said that English **was** an international language.

Be careful! Remember that when the reporting verb is in the present tense, the verb tense in indirect speech does not change.
They **say** a big storm **is** expected to arrive tomorrow morning.
Don't say: They say a big storm ~~was~~ ...

On a separate sheet of paper, write each direct speech statement in indirect speech. Change the verb in the indirect speech only if necessary.

1 Last Friday my husband said, "I'm going to pick up some things at the pharmacy before the storm."

2 Last year my parents said, "We're going to Spain on vacation this year."

3 She told them, "This year's flu shot is not entirely protective against the flu."

4 He just said, "The danger of a flood is over."

5 We always say, "It's easier to take the train than drive."

6 When I was a child, my parents told me, "It's really important to get a good education."

7 The National Weather Service is saying, "Tonight's weather is terrible."

8 Your parents just told me, "We want to leave for the shelter immediately."

UNIT 6 Lesson 1

Expressing the future: review

The present continuous
My tooth has been killing me all week. I**'m calling** the dentist tomorrow.
What are you doing this afternoon? I**'m going** to the beach.

The simple present tense
The office is usually open until 9:00, but it **closes** at 6:00 tomorrow.

Modals should, could, ought to, may, might, have to, and can
You **could** catch the next bus. We **should** call her next week.

A Read each sentence. Check the sentences that have future meaning.

☐ **1** Hannah is studying English this month.

☐ **2** Nancy studies English in the evening.

☐ **3** You should call me tomorrow.

☐ **4** He might have time to see you later.

☐ **5** My parents are arriving at 10:00.

☐ **6** I'm taking my daughter out for dinner tonight.

☐ **7** I'm eating dinner with my daughter. Can I call you back?

☐ **8** The class always starts at 2:00 and finishes at 4:00.

☐ **9** We may stay another week in Paris.

The future with will and be going to: review

Use **will** or **be going to** to make a prediction or to indicate that something in the future will be true. There is no difference in meaning.
Getting a new car **will cost** a lot of money.   Getting a new car **is going to cost** a lot of money.

Use **be going to** to express a plan.
My tooth has been killing me all week. I**'m going to call** a dentist. NOT I will call a dentist.

Be careful! **Will** is also used for willingness. This use of **will** doesn't have a future meaning.
Be going to cannot be used for willingness.
A: Is it true that you **won't go** to the dentist?
B: I**'ll go** to the dentist, but I don't like fillings. NOT I'm going to go…

B Complete the conversations, using <u>will</u> or <u>be going to</u>.

1 A: Would you like to go running in the park? I _____ in about half an hour.
leave

   B: That sounds great. I _____ you there.
meet

2 A: It's midnight. Why are you still reading?

   B: We _____ a test tomorrow.
have

3 A: Do you have plans for tomorrow?

   B: Yes. I _____ a chiropractor for the first time.
see

4 A: I hope you can come tomorrow night. We'd really like you to be there.

   B: OK. I _____ .
come

5 A: I'm thinking about getting a new laptop.

   B: Really? Well, I _____ you mine. I love it.
show

UNIT 6 *Lesson 2*

Regrets about the past: <u>wish</u> + the past perfect; <u>should have</u> and <u>ought to have</u>

<u>Wish</u> + the past perfect
   I wish I **had married** later. And I wish I **hadn't married** Celine!
   Do you wish you **had bought** that car when it was available?

<u>Should have</u> and <u>ought to have</u> + past participle
   <u>Ought to have</u> has the same meaning as **<u>should have</u>**.
   I should have married later = I ought to have married later.
   I shouldn't have married Celine. = I ought not to have married Celine.

Note: American English speakers use <u>should have</u> instead of <u>ought to have</u> in negative statements and in questions.

On a separate sheet of paper, rewrite the statements and questions, changing <u>wish</u> + the past perfect to <u>should have</u> or <u>ought to have</u>.

1 She wishes she had had children. (ought to)

2 Do you wish you had studied Swahili? (should)

3 I wish I had gone to New Zealand instead of Australia. (ought to)

4 Do you wish you had taken the job at the embassy? (should)

5 I wish I hadn't studied law. (should)

UNIT 7 *Lesson 1*

Adjective clauses: common errors

Remember:
Use the relative pronouns <u>who</u> or <u>that</u> for adjectives that describe people. Use <u>that</u> for adjective clauses that describe things.
   Don't say: Feijoada is a dish ~~who~~ is famous in Brazil.

Don't use a subject pronoun after the relative pronoun.
   Don't say: Feijoada is a dish that ~~it~~ is famous in Brazil.

A On a separate sheet of paper, combine the two sentences into one, making the second sentence an adjective clause. Use <u>who</u> whenever it is possible. When it isn't possible, use <u>that</u>. Follow the example.

The hotel clerk was very helpful. / He recommended the restaurant.

The hotel clerk who recommended the restaurant was very helpful.

1 My cousin lives in New Zealand. / She called today.

2 We have a meeting every morning. / It begins at 9:30.

3 The celebration is exciting. / It takes place in spring.

4 The teacher is not very formal. / She teaches the grammar class.

5 Patients might prefer homeopathy. / They want to avoid strong medications.

6 The copy shop is closed on weekends. / It offers express service.

7 The hotel is very expensive. / It has three swimming pools.

8 Do you like the teacher? / He teaches advanced English.

Reflexive pronouns

Reflexive pronouns	
myself	itself
yourself	ourselves
himself	yourselves
herself	themselves

A reflexive pronoun should always agree with the subject of the verb.

People really enjoy **themselves** at Brazil's Carnaval celebrations.

My sister made **herself** sick from eating so much.

Common expressions with reflexive pronouns

believe in oneself	If you **believe in yourself**, you can do anything.
enjoy oneself	We **enjoyed ourselves** on our vacation.
feel sorry for oneself	Don't sit around **feeling sorry for yourself**.
help oneself (to something)	Please **help yourselves** to dessert.
hurt oneself	Paul **hurt himself** when he tried to move the fridge.
give oneself (something)	I wanted to **give myself** a gift, so I got a massage.
introduce oneself	Why don't you **introduce yourselves** to your new neighbors?
be proud of oneself	She was **proud of herself** for getting the job.
take care of oneself	You should **take** better **care of yourself**.
talk to oneself	I sometimes **talk to myself** when I feel nervous.
teach oneself (to do something)	Nick **taught himself** to use a computer.
tell oneself (something)	I always **tell myself** I'm not going to eat dessert, but I do.
work for oneself	Oscar left the company and now he **works for himself**.

B Complete the sentences with reflexive pronouns.

1 My brother and his wife really enjoyed _____ on their vacation.

2 My uncle has been teaching _____ how to cook.

3 The food was so terrific that I helped _____ to some more.

4 Instead of staying at home and feeling sorry for _____ after the accident, I stayed in touch with all my friends.

5 I hope your sister's been taking good care of _____.

6 I was too shy to introduce _____ to anyone at the party.

7 Mr. Yu hurt _____ while lighting firecrackers for the Chinese New Year.

C Complete each sentence with one of the common expressions with reflexive pronouns. Then add two more sentences of your own.

1 When did your brother _____ how to play the guitar?

2 You'd better tell your daughter to stop playing near the stove or she'll _____.

3 I really hope you _____ when you're on vacation.

4 _____

5 _____

By + reflexive pronouns

Use **by** with a reflexive pronoun to mean "alone."
You cannot put on a kimono **by yourself**. You need help.
Students cannot learn to speak English **by themselves**. They need practice with others in English.

D Complete each sentence with **by** and a reflexive pronoun.

1 Very young children shouldn't be allowed to play outside _____.

2 Did your father go to the store _____?

3 When did you learn to fix a computer _____?

4 We got tired of waiting for a table at the restaurant, so we found one _____.

Reciprocal pronouns: _each other_ and _one another_

Each other and **one another** have the same meaning, but **one another** is more formal.
People give **each other** (or **one another**) gifts.
Friends send **each other** (or **one another**) cards.

> **Be careful!**
> Reciprocal pronouns don't have the same meaning as reflexive pronouns.
> They looked at **themselves**. (Each person looked in a mirror or at a photo.)
> They looked at **each other**. (Each person looked at the other person.)

E On a separate sheet of paper, rewrite each underlined phrase, using a reciprocal pronoun. Then add one sentence of your own. Follow the example.

On Christmas, in many places in the world, people give and receive presents.

On Christmas, in many places in the world, people give each other presents.

1 On New Year's Eve, in New York City, people wait in Times Square for midnight to come so they can kiss other people and wish other people a happy new year.

2 During the Thai holiday _Songkran_, people throw water at other people on the street.

3 During the Tomato Festival In Buñol, Spain, people have a lot of fun throwing tomatoes at other people for about two hours.

4 After a day of fasting during Ramadan, Muslims around the world invite other people home to have something to eat that evening.

5 (Your own sentence)

UNIT 7 Lesson 2

Adjective clauses: _who_ and _whom_ in formal English

In formal written or spoken English, use **who** for subject relative pronouns and **whom** for object relative pronouns.

	subject
The singer was terrible.	+ **He** sang in the restaurant.
The singer	**who sang in the restaurant** was terrible.

	object
The singer was terrible.	+ We heard **him** last night.
The singer	**whom we heard last night** was terrible.

> **Remember:** An object relative pronoun can be omitted.
> The singer we heard last night was terrible.

Complete each (formal) sentence with **who** or **whom**.

1 The concierge _____ works at that hotel is very helpful.

2 The man _____ I met on the plane has invited us to lunch.

3 The manager _____ lives in Singapore may apply for the job.

4 I'm very satisfied with the dentist _____ you recommended.

5 The guests _____ we invited to the dinner were an hour late.

6 The sales representative _____ you are going to call speaks English.

7 The singer _____ you told me about is performing tonight.

8 My friend _____ works at the bank can help you.

9 Is your colleague someone _____ I can ask to help me?

Real and unreal conditionals: review

Remember: Conditional sentences have two clauses: an <u>if</u>-clause and a result clause.

- Real (or "factual") conditionals express the present or future results of real conditions.

   Present or everlasting results: Use the present of <u>be</u> or the simple present tense in both clauses.
   If I **speak** slowly, people **understand** me.
   If the temperature of water **rises** above 100 degrees Celsius, it **turns** to steam.

   Future results: Use the present of <u>be</u> or the simple present tense in the <u>if</u>-clause. Use a future form (future with <u>will</u> or present continuous for the future) in the result clause.
   If I'm late, I'**ll disturb** the others at the meeting.

   Remember: The order of the clauses can be reversed. It's customary to use a comma after the <u>if</u>-clause when it comes first.
   If you **buy** a smart phone, you **won't need** both a cell phone and a PDA.
   You **won't need** both a cell phone and a PDA if you **buy** a smart phone.

   Remember: Don't use a future form in the <u>if</u>-clause. Don't say: If I ~~will be~~ late, I'll disturb the others at the meeting.

- Unreal conditionals express the results of conditions that don't exist. Use the simple past tense or <u>were</u> in the <u>if</u>-clause. Use <u>would</u> + a base form in the result clause. The order of the clauses can be reversed.
   If I **bought** a more economical car, I **wouldn't worry** so much about the price of gasoline.
   If he **were** here, he **would tell** us about his trip.

   Remember: Don't use the conditional in the <u>if</u>-clause. Don't say: If he ~~would be~~ here, he would tell us about his trip.

A Correct the errors in the conditional sentences.

1 If you will take a good picture, it can preserve memories of times you might forget.

2 If I was you, I would send them an e-mail right away.

3 If you would go out today, you'll need an umbrella.

4 Most people would eat healthy food if they understand the consequences of eating too much junk food.

5 These speakers will be OK if you used them in a smaller room.

6 If the weather will be better, I'd go for a swim.

7 If I would have a chance, I would work shorter hours.

8 Will you ride a bicycle to work if your car broke down?

9 What would you do if I would ask you to make dinner?

10 He won't eat at that restaurant if they would tell him he had to wear formal clothes.

Clauses after <u>wish</u>

Use <u>were</u> or the simple past tense after <u>wish</u> to express a regret about something that's not true now.
   I **wish** my laptop **were** top-of-the-line. (But it's not top-of-the-line.)
   I **wish** I **had** a Brew Rite digital coffee maker. (But I don't have one.)

Remember: Use the past perfect after <u>wish</u> to express a regret about something that was not true in the past.
   Sean **wishes** he **hadn't sold** his car. (But he did sell it.)
   Sean **wished** he **hadn't sold** his car. (But he did.)

Use the conditional (<u>would</u> or <u>could</u> + a base form) after <u>wish</u> to express a desire in the present that something will occur in the future or on an ongoing basis.
   I **wish** it **would rain**. (a desire for a future occurrence)
   I **wish** it **would rain** more often. (a desire for something to occur on an ongoing basis)

Use <u>would</u> and a base form after <u>wished</u> to express a wish one had in the past for a future occurrence.
   Yesterday I **wished** it **would rain**, but it didn't. (a past wish for a future occurrence)

B **Complete each statement or question with the correct form of the verb.**

1 I wish my favorite author _____ a new book. I've read all her old books so many times.
      write

2 Pat wished she _____ more time test-driving cars before she bought that SUV.
      spend

3 Most people wish they _____ rich.
      be

4 I wish it _____ possible for me to get a better camera when I bought this one.
      be

5 They wished they _____ sooner that their computer couldn't be fixed.
      know

6 When I was a child, my parents wished I _____ a doctor.
      become

7 Do you wish you _____ a more comfortable car for the trip tomorrow?
      have

8 Don't they wish they _____ German?
      study

9 I wish I _____ a mechanic. My car keeps breaking down.
      marry

Unless in conditional sentences

You can use <u>unless</u> (in place of <u>if</u> + <u>not</u>) in negative <u>if</u>-clauses.
   Unless they buy a freezer, they'll have to go shopping every day. (= If they don't buy a freezer,...)
   She wouldn't go for a long drive **unless** she had a cell phone with her. (= ...if she didn't have a cell phone with her.)
   Martin doesn't buy electronics **unless** they're state-of-the-art. (= ... if they're not state-of-the-art.)

C **On a separate sheet of paper, rewrite the sentences, changing <u>if not</u> statements to <u>unless</u> and making any necessary changes. Follow the example.**

If you don't buy the Brew Rite coffee maker, you'll have to spend a lot more money on another brand.

Unless you buy the Brew Rite coffee maker, you'll have to spend a lot more money on another brand.

1 If you aren't in a hurry, you should walk.

2 If you don't care about special features, you shouldn't consider getting the top-of-the-line model.

3 She won't go running in the park if her friends don't go with her.

4 Claire won't buy a car if it doesn't have a high-tech sound system.

UNIT 8 *Lesson 2*

The unreal conditional: variety of forms

Unreal conditional sentences can have a variety of active and passive forms in either clause.
   If she **had worn** a seat belt, she **wouldn't have been** hurt.
   If the car **had been totaled**, he **would have bought** a new one.
   If the automobile **hadn't been invented**, we **would** still **be using** horses.
   If horses **were** still **being used**, our high-speed highway system **would never have been created**.
   If Marie Claire **were getting** married today, she **wouldn't marry** Joe.
   If she **had married** Joe, she **would have children** today.

On a separate sheet of paper, complete the following unreal conditional sentences in your own way, using active and passive forms. Refer to the presentation on page 135 for some possibilities.

1 If I were elected ruler of a country, . . .

2 The car would have been invented earlier if . . .

3 If I were looking for a high-tech smart phone, . . .

4 If this laptop had been available when I was looking for one, . . .

5 . . . , I wouldn't be studying English now.

6 If I were going to take a commercial space flight today, . . .

UNIT 9 *Lesson 1*

Count and non-count nouns: review and extension

Count nouns name things that can be counted individually. They have singular and plural forms.

a president / presidents	a liberal / liberals	a candidate / candidates
a government / governments	an election / elections	a monarchy / monarchies

Non-count nouns name things that are not counted individually. They don't have singular or plural forms and they are not preceded by a or an. To express a specific quantity of a non-count noun, use unit expressions.

a piece of news	a cup of tea	a kilo of rice	a time of peace	an act of justice

Many nouns can be used as count or non-count nouns, but the meaning is different.

She studied **government** at the university. (= an academic subject)
That country has had four **governments** in ten years. (= a group of people who rule the country)

Democracy is the best form of government. (= a type of government)
After the revolution, the country became **a democracy**. (= a country with a democratic system)

I love **chicken**. (the food, in general)
I bought **a chicken**. (the actual whole bird)

She has blond **hair**. (in general = all of her hair)
She got **a hair** in her eye. (= one individual strand of hair)

Complete each sentence with the correct form of each noun.

1 The government has made _____ with the economic situation.
                 progress

2 They've given a lot of _____ to making the banks stable.
             importance

3 Unfortunately, _____ changed the law.
          radical

4 _____ can only come if people stop making war.
     peace

5 _____ don't favor extreme change.
    moderate

6 He's _____ who would like to outlaw freedom of speech.
      reactionary

7 If I could give you one piece of _____, it would be to vote.
          advice

8 If more people don't find _____, people will elect a different president.
       work

9 Some _____ are more liberal than others.
    government

10 It's impossible to end all _____.
      poverty

Gerunds and infinitives: review of form and usage

Form
Gerunds: A gerund is a noun formed from a verb. All gerunds end in -ing. To form a gerund, add -ing to the base form of a verb.

discuss → discuss**ing**

If the base form ends in a silent -e, drop the -e and add -ing.

vote → vot**ing**

In verbs of one syllable, if the last three letters are a consonant-vowel-consonant* (CVC) sequence, double the last consonant and then add -ing to the base form.

C V C

s i t → sitting

> * Vowels = a, e, i, o, u
> * Consonants = b, c, d, f, g, h, j, k, l, m, n, p, q, r, s, t, v, w, x, y, z

BUT: If the base form of the verb ends in -w, -x, or -y, don't double the final consonant.

blow → blowing   **fix** → fixing   **say** → saying

If a base form has more than one syllable and ends in a consonant-vowel-consonant sequence, double the last consonant only if the spoken stress is on the last syllable.

permit → permitting   BUT   order → ordering

Infinitives: An infinitive is also a verbal noun. It is formed with to + the base form of a verb.

elect → **to elect**   persuade → **to persuade**

Usage
Gerunds can be subjects, objects, and subject complements within sentences.

Discussing politics is my favorite activity. (subject)
I love **reading** about government. (direct object of verb <u>love</u>)
I read a book about **voting**. (object of preposition <u>about</u>)
My favorite pastime is **watching** TV news. (subject complement after <u>be</u>)

Infinitives function as subjects, direct objects, and subject complements.

To hang out all day discussing politics would be my favorite weekend activity. (subject)
I love **to guess** who's going to win elections. (direct object of verb <u>love</u>)
My greatest dream for the future is **to work** in the government. (subject complement after <u>be</u>)

A Using the sentences in the box above as a model, write pairs of sentences on a separate sheet of paper, using the gerunds and infinitives in the two ways shown.

1 voting
   a (as the subject of a sentence)
   b (as a direct object)

2 smoking
   a (as a direct object)
   b (as an object of the preposition <u>to</u>)

3 censoring
   a (as the object of the preposition <u>of</u>)
   b (as a subject complement)

4 to permit
   a (as the subject of a sentence)
   b (as a direct object)

5 to lower
   a (as a direct object)
   b (as a subject of a sentence)

Gerunds and infinitives: review of usage after certain verbs

Certain verbs are followed by gerunds:
avoid, can't stand, discuss, dislike, enjoy, feel like, (don't) mind, practice, quit, suggest

Other verbs are followed by infinitives:
agree, choose, decide, expect, hope, learn, need, plan, seem, want, wish, would like

Other verbs can be followed by either a gerund or an infinitive:
begin, continue, hate, like, love, prefer

> For a review of gerunds and infinitives, open **Reference Charts** on your *ActiveBook* Self-Study Disc.

B Complete the paragraph with gerunds or infinitives. When either a gerund or an infinitive is correct, fill in the blank with both forms.

I hope _____ some positive changes in my life, and I would like _____ right away.
1 make 2 start
I have observed that a lot of people enjoy _____ about the political situation, but they don't like
3 complain
_____ anything about it. They love _____ the news and _____ they care
4 do 5 watch 6 say
about all the poor people who don't have enough to eat, but they don't feel like _____ anything to
7 do
change the situation. They worry about poverty, but they don't mind _____ money on stupid things
8 waste
they don't need _____ . Well, I'm sick of _____ about how people are suffering, and I've
9 have 10 read
agreed _____ a political action group. I simply hate _____ anything!
11 join 12 not do

UNIT 10 Lesson 1

Prepositions of place: more usage

It's **in** {
Cheju Province.
the Rocky Mountains.
the Central Valley.
the Sahara Desert.
the Atlantic Ocean.
the state of Jalisco.
}

It's **on** {
the Nicoya Peninsula.
Easter Island.
the Hudson River.
Coronado Bay.
the coast.
Lake Placid.
the Gulf of Aqaba.
}

{
It's in the central part
It's southwest
It's about 50 kilometers north
} **of** Madrid.

A Write the correct prepositions of place.

1 Pisco is _____ the Pacific coast of Peru.

2 Tianjin, in China, is _____ Hebei Province.

3 Desaguadero is _____ Lake Titicaca in Bolivia.

4 The island of Bahrain is _____ the Persian Gulf.

5 Cabimas is _____ Lake Maracaibo in Venezuela.

6 Sapporo is _____ Hokkaido Island in Japan.

7 Riobamba is _____ the Pastaza River in Ecuador.

8 Taiwan's Jade Mountain National Park is east _____ the city of Alishan.

9 Fengkang is _____ the southern part _____ Taiwan.

10 The city of Budapest, Hungary, is _____ the Danube River.

11 Denmark is north _____ Germany.

12 The capital of Chile, Santiago, is located _____ the Central Valley.

Proper nouns: capitalization

Capitalize names of:

places	Bolivia, the United Kingdom, Kyoto
languages / nationalities	French, Korean, Arabic
buildings and public places	the Paramount Theater, the Tower of London, the Golden Gate Bridge
organizations	the U.N., the World Bank, Amnesty International
names and titles	Mary, Mary Smith, Dr. Mary Smith
days / months / holidays	Monday, January, the Moon Festival
religions	Christianity, Islam, Buddhism
historic times or events	the Cold War, the Middle Ages, the Edo Period

When a proper noun has more than one word, each word is capitalized, except for articles (the) and prepositions (of).

Panama City
the University of Buenos Aires

the Gulf of Aqaba
Niagara Falls

the City of Chicago
the Bay of Biscayne

Capitalize all the words of a title, except for articles and prepositions that have fewer than four letters. If an article or a preposition is the first word of a title, capitalize it.

The Story of English
The International Herald Tribune

Looking Back on My Life
I Know Why the Caged Bird Sings

B On a separate sheet of paper, rewrite each sentence with correct capitalization. Follow the example.

i'm reading one hundred years of solitude.

I'm reading One Hundred Years of Solitude.

1 my cousins are studying french.

2 the leaning tower of pisa is in northern italy.

3 it's on the southern coast of australia.

4 i visit the city museum of art every saturday.

5 my uncle jack works for the united nations.

6 the channel tunnel between england and france was completed in 1994.

7 she graduated from the university of washington.

8 we liked the movie about the great wall of china.

9 my son is in the college of sciences.

10 his father speaks korean and japanese fluently

11 their grandson was born last march.

Proper nouns: use of the

When a proper noun includes the word of, use the.

with the	without the
the Republic of Korea	Korea
the Gulf of Mexico	Mexico City
the Kingdom of Thailand	Thailand

When a proper noun uses a political word such as republic, empire, or kingdom, use the.

the United Kingdom   the British Empire   the Malagasy Republic

When a proper noun is plural, use the.

the Philippines	the United States
the Netherlands	the Andes Mountains

When a proper noun includes a geographical word such as ocean, desert, or river, use the. BUT do not use the with the following geographical words: lake, bay, mountain, island, or park.

with the	without the
the Atlantic Ocean	Crystal Lake
the Atacama Desert	Hudson Bay
the Yangtze River	Hainan Island
the Iberian Peninsula	Ueno Park
the Persian Gulf	Yellow Mountain

When words like east or southwest are used as the name of a geographical area, use the. Do not use the when they are used as adjectives.

with the	without the
the Middle East	Western Europe
the Far East	East Timor
the West	Northern Ireland

When a proper noun includes a word that is a kind of organization or educational group, use the. Do not use the with a university or college (unless the name uses of).

with the	without the
the International Language Institute	Columbia College
the United Nations	Chubu University
the World Health Organization	
the University of Adelaide	

Do not use the with acronyms.

U.C.L.A. (the University of California, Los Angeles)

NATO (the North Atlantic Treaty Organization)

OPEC (the Organization of Petroleum Exporting Countries)

C Correct the errors in the following sentences. Explain your answers.

1 When she went to the Malaysia, she brought her husband with her.

2 A lot of people from United States teach English here.

3 The Haiti is the closest neighbor to Dominican Republic.

4 When we arrived in the Berlin, I was very excited.

5 The Jordan is a country in Middle East.

6 I introduced our visitors to University of Riyadh.

7 I lived in People's Republic of China for about two years.

8 Mr. Yan is a student at College of Arts and Sciences.

9 She is the director of English Language Institute.

10 She's the most famous actress in Netherlands.

11 He's interested in cultures in Middle East.

12 The Poland was one of the first countries in the Eastern Europe to change to democracy.

UNIT 10 Lesson 2

Infinitives with *enough*

You can use an infinitive after an adjective and **enough** to give an explanation.
She's **old enough** to vote.   He's not **busy enough** to complain.

Be careful! **Too** comes before an adjective, but **enough** comes after an adjective.
It's **too far** to walk.
It isn't **close enough** to walk. NOT It isn't ~~enough close~~ to walk.

A On a separate sheet of paper, complete each statement in your own way, using an infinitive.

1 He's tall enough . . .

2 He isn't strong enough . . .

3 She's thirsty enough . . .

4 She isn't hungry enough . . .

5 The movie was interesting enough . . .

6 The movie wasn't exciting enough . . .

B On a separate sheet of paper, write ten sentences, using your choice of adjectives from the box. Write five using _too_ and an infinitive and five using _enough_ and an infinitive.

early	heavy	important	old	young	long
expensive	high	loud	sick	scary	short

Writing Booster

The Writing Booster is optional. It is intended to orient students to the elements of good writing. Each unit's Writing Booster is focused both on a skill and its application to the Writing topic from the Review page.

UNIT 1 *Formal e-mail etiquette*

Social e-mails between friends are informal and have almost no rules. Friends don't mind seeing spelling or grammar errors and use "emoticons" and abbreviations.

Emoticons	**Abbreviations**
☺ = I'm smiling.	LOL = "Laughing out loud"
☹ = I'm not happy.	LMK = "Let me know"
	BTW = "By the way"
	IMHO = "In my humble opinion"

However, because e-mail is so fast and convenient, it is commonly used in business communication and between people who have a more formal relationship. When writing a more formal e-mail, it is not acceptable to use the same informal style you would use when communicating with a friend.

For formal e-mails . . .

Do:
- Use title and last name and a colon in the salutation, unless you are already on a first-name basis:
  Dear Mr. Samuelson:
  Dear Dr. Kent:
  If you are on a first-name basis, it's appropriate to address the person with his or her first name:
  Dear Marian:
- Write in complete sentences, not fragments or run-on sentences.
- Check and correct your spelling.
- Use capital and lowercase letters correctly.
- Use correct punctuation.
- Use a complimentary close as in a formal letter, such as:
  Sincerely, Cordially, Thank you, Thanks so much.
- End with your name, even though it's already in the e-mail message bar.

Don't:
- Use emoticons.
- Use abbreviations such as "LOL" or "u" for "you."
- Use all lowercase letters.
- Date the e-mail the way you would a written letter. (The date is already in the headings bar.)

A Circle all the formal e-mail etiquette errors in the following e-mail to a business associate. Then explain your reasons.

Glenn, it was nice to see u yesterday at the meeting. I was wondering if we could continue the meeting sometime next week. Maybe on Tuesday at your place? There's still a lot we need 2 discus. I know you love long meetings LMK if u wanna change the time.

B Guidance for Writing (page 12) Use the do's and don'ts to check the two e-mail messages you wrote for Exercise D.

UNIT 2 *Comparisons and contrasts*

COMPARISONS: Use this language to compare two things:

To introduce similarities
- **be alike**
  Herbal medicine and homeopathy **are alike** in some ways.
- **be similar to**
  Homeopathy **is similar to** conventional medicine in some ways.

To provide details
- **both**
  Both herbal medicine and homeopathy are based on plants. / Herbal medicine and homeopathy are **both** based on plants.
- **and . . . too**
  Herbal medicine is based on plants **and** homeopathy is **too**.
- **and . . . (not) either**
  Herbal medicine doesn't use medications **and** homeopathy **doesn't either**.
- **also**
  Many of the medications in conventional medicine **also** come from plants.
- **as well**
  Many of the medications in conventional medicine come from plants **as well**.
- **Likewise,**
  Herbs offer an alternative to conventional medications. **Likewise,** homeopathy offers a different approach.
- **Similarly,**
  Similarly, homeopathy offers a different approach.

CONTRASTS: Use this language to contrast two things:

<u>To introduce differences</u>
- **be different from**
  Conventional medicine **is different from** acupuncture in a number of ways.

<u>To provide details</u>
- **but**
  Herbal medicine treats illness with herbs, **but** acupuncture mainly treats illness with needles.
- **while / whereas**
  Herbal medicine treats illness with herbs **while** (or **whereas**) acupuncture treats illness with needles. OR **While** (or **Whereas**) herbal medicine treats illness with herbs, acupuncture treats illness with needles.
- **unlike**
  Spiritual healing involves taking responsibility for one's own healing, **unlike** conventional medicine. OR **Unlike** conventional medicine, spiritual healing involves taking responsibility for one's own healing.
- **However,**
  Conventional doctors routinely treat heart disease with bypass surgery. **However,** acupuncturists take a different approach.
- **In contrast,**
  Herbal doctors treat illnesses with teas made from plants. **In contrast,** conventional doctors use medicines and surgery.
- **On the other hand,**
  Conventional medicine is based on modern scientific research. **On the other hand,** herbal therapy is based on centuries of common knowledge.

A **On a separate sheet of paper, make comparisons, using the cues in parentheses.**

1 There's nothing scarier than having a toothache while traveling. Feeling short of breath while on the road can be a frightening experience. (likewise)

2 Many painkillers can be bought without a prescription. Many antihistamines can be bought without a prescription. (both)

3 A broken tooth requires a visit to the dentist. A lost filling requires a visit to the dentist. (and . . . too)

4 You may have to wait for the results of an X-ray. The results of a blood test may not be ready for several days. (similarly)

5 An X-ray doesn't take much time to do. A blood test doesn't take much time to do. (and... not / either)

B **On a separate sheet of paper, make contrasts, using the cues in parentheses.**

1 If you feel pain in your back, you can try taking a painkiller. If you have pain in your chest, you should see a doctor. (on the other hand)

2 Homeopathy is fairly common in Europe. It is not as popular in the United States. (while)

3 Spiritual healing uses the mind or religious faith to treat illnesses. Other types of treatments do not. (unlike)

4 Conventional medicine and acupuncture have been used for thousands of years. Homeopathy was only introduced in the late 18th century. (whereas)

5 Many people choose conventional medicine first when they need medical help. About 80% of the world's population uses some form of herbal therapy for their regular health care. (however)

C **Guidance for Writing (page 24) On a separate sheet of paper, write three statements that show similarities in the two medical treatments you chose to write about in Exercise E and three statements that contrast them. Use the language of comparison and contrast in each statement. Use these statements in your writing.**

UNIT 3 *Supporting an opinion with personal examples*

Use these expressions to state your opinions. Follow the punctuation style in the examples.

- **In my opinion,**
  In my opinion, there's nothing wrong with being a procrastinator. People just have different personalities.
- **To me,**
  To me, it's better to be well-organized. Being a procrastinator keeps a person from getting things done.
- **From my point of view,**
  From my point of view, if you aren't well-organized, you're going to have a lot of problems in life.
- **I believe**
  I believe that people who are procrastinators have other strengths such as creativity.
- **I find**
  I find being well-organized helps a person get more done.

Note: All of these expressions can be used either at the beginning of a sentence or at the end. Use a comma before the expression when you use it at the end of a sentence.

There's nothing wrong with being a procrastinator, **in my opinion**.
Being well-organized helps a person get more done, **I find**.

Use personal examples to make your opinions clear and interesting to readers.

- **For example,**
  I'm usually on time in everything I do. **For example,** I always pay my bills on time.
- **For instance,**
  My brother is usually on time in everything he does, but sometimes he isn't. **For instance,** last week he completely forgot to get our mother a birthday gift.
- **…, such as …**
  There are a few things I tend to put off, **such as** paying bills and studying for tests.
- **Whenever**
  Some people have a hard time paying their bills on time. **Whenever** my husband receives a bill, he puts it on the shelf and forgets about it.
- **Every time**
  Every time I forget to pay a bill, I feel terrible.
- **When I was …**
  I had to learn how to be well-organized. **When I was** a child, my parents did everything for me.

> **Be careful!**
> Do not use for example or for instance to combine sentences.
> Don't write: I'm usually on time for everything I do, for example, I always pay my bills on time.

> Remember:
> Use a comma before such as when it introduces a dependent clause.

A On a separate sheet of paper, write a sentence expressing your personal opinion in response to each of the following questions.

1 Do you think children should study the arts in school?

2 Do you think extroverts are better people than introverts?

3 Do you think it's OK to wear casual clothes in an office?

B On a separate sheet of paper, provide a personal example for each of the following statements.

1 I'm (I'm not) a very well-organized person.

2 Some (None) of the people I know procrastinate.

3 I always (don't always) pay my bills on time.

4 I've always (never) had a hard time doing things on time.

C Guidance for Writing (page 36) On a separate sheet of paper, state your opinion on the topic in Exercise D. Then list at least five personal examples to support your view. Use the examples in your writing.

UNIT 4 *Summarizing*

A good summary provides only the main ideas of a much longer reading, movie, or event. It should not include lots of details. Here are two effective ways to write a summary:

1 **Answer basic information questions:** For a longer reading, one approach to writing a summary is to think about the answers to basic questions of: Who?, What?, When?, Where?, Why?, and How?

2 **Focus on main ideas instead of details:** For a shorter reading, identify the main ideas. Sentences that are main ideas provide enough information to tell the story. After you have identified the sentences that express the main ideas, rewrite them in your own words.

> **Some basic information questions:**
> **Who was the book about?**
> The book I read is about Benito Juárez.
> **Who was Juárez?**
> Juárez was the president of Mexico from 1867 to 1872.
> **Why was he important?**
> He restored the Republic and modernized the country.

A Practice answering basic information questions. Think of a movie you really like. On a separate sheet of paper, write any answers you can to the following questions.

1 Who is the movie about?

2 When does the movie take place?

3 Where does the movie take place?

4 In three to five sentences, what is the movie about?

5 What actors are in the movie? Who is the director?

6 (Add your own information question)

B Practice focusing on main ideas. In the following article, underline any sentences you think are main ideas. Cross out any sentences that you think are details.

Thirty years ago, most people in the United States, Canada, and Europe didn't think about what to wear to work in an office. Men always wore suits and ties. Women wore suits or conservative skirt outfits. But in the 1990's, that started to change.

It began with "casual Fridays." During the summer, some companies invited their employees to "dress down," or wear more casual clothes to work on Fridays. The policy quickly became popular with employees. After this, it didn't take long for employees to start dressing more casually every day of the week.

Many employees welcomed the new dress policy and the more comfortable work environment that came with it. Etiquette had definitely changed, and suits and ties were rarely seen in many offices. Some employees went as far as wearing jeans, T-shirts, and sneakers to the office.

Then some people began to change their minds about casual dress at work. Many managers felt that casual dress had led to casual attitudes toward work. Now the etiquette for dress in many companies is beginning to change back again.

> After you have completed Exercise B, read this summary of the article. How does it compare with the sentences you underlined in the article?
>
> Thirty years ago, most people in the United States, Canada, and Europe didn't think about what to wear to work in an office. But in the 1990's, that started to change. During the summer, some companies invited their employees to "dress down," or wear more casual clothes to work on Fridays. Then some people began to change their minds about casual dress at work. Now the etiquette for dress in many companies is beginning to change back again.

C Guidance for Writing (page 48) Answer each question if you can. If you cannot answer a question, answer the next one. Then use your answers to write the summary within your review.

1 What is the title of the reading material you chose?

2 Who is the writer?

3 Who is it about?

4 What is it about?

5 Where does it take place?

6 When does it take place?

7 Why was it written?

8 Why is it important?

9 Did you like it? Why or why not?

10 Would you recommend it to others? Why or why not?

UNIT 5 *Organizing detail statements by order of importance*

One way to organize supporting details within a paragraph is by **order of importance**, usually beginning with the most important and ending with the least important. Or, if you wish, it is possible to reverse the order, beginning with the least important and building to the most important.

Imagine you are writing an essay about how to prepare for a trip. Use words and expressions that indicate the relative importance of details to the reader.

First, [or **First and most important,**] make sure your passport is up-to-date. Nothing can be worse than arriving at the airport and not being able to get on the plane.

Second, [or **Next,** or **Following that,**] check the weather for your destination. This will ensure that you bring the right clothes. It's terrible to arrive somewhere and find out that the weather is unusually cold for this time of year. The last thing you want to do is to have to go shopping!

Last, [or **Finally,**] write a list of important phone numbers and e-mail addresses of people you have to contact. It can be hard to get that information if you are out of your own country.

> Following are two ways to construct the paragraph:
>
> 1 Write a topic sentence stating the main idea of the paragraph and then begin describing the details in order of importance.
>
> The severity of an earthquake is determined by several factors. **First and most important** is the magnitude of the quake. Really strong earthquakes cause lots of damage, even to well-constructed buildings, no matter where or when they occur. Earthquakes with a Richter reading of 9 or over are uniformly catastrophic. **The second most important factor** is location, …etc.
>
> 2 Write a topic sentence that states the details in the order of importance.
>
> The severity of an earthquake is determined by four factors, in order of importance: magnitude, location, quality of construction, and timing. The magnitude of an earthquake is by far the most significant factor in its destructive power… etc.

A On a separate sheet of paper, rewrite the following paragraph, inserting words to indicate the relative importance of each item.

> Here are some things not to forget when preparing for an emergency. Call your relatives who live in other places, telling them where you are so they don't worry. Have a discussion with all family members about the importance of listening to emergency broadcasts. Keep a supply of blankets and warm jackets in case of power outages or flooding. Be sure to follow all emergency instructions carefully: your life and the life of your family could depend on it.

B Guidance for Writing (page 60) Look at the list of supplies and resources. Number them in order of their importance for the emergency you chose. Write notes about why each one is important. Use your notes to help you write about how to prepare for your emergency.

Type of emergency: _____

Supplies and resources	Notes
non-perishable food:	
bottled water	
batteries	
cell phones	
smart phones	
GPS devices	
medications	
phone numbers	

UNIT 6   *Dividing an essay into topics*

Look at the picture in the Oral Review on page 73. The picture tells the story of the lives of Michael and Carlota. It is divided into three topics, each with a date and a topic heading. The headings help the viewer see at a glance how the story will be organized.

Similarly, if a piece of writing contains more than one section or topic, it is sometimes helpful to include **topic headings** each time a new section begins. Each topic heading signals the topic of the paragraph or section In the way a table of contents tells a reader what the sections of a book will be.

A Read the following short biography of famous Dutch painter Vincent Van Gogh. Write your own topic headings to divide the biography into sections.

Early Life

Vincent Van Gogh was born in a small village in Holland on March 30, 1853. He was an introverted child and he didn't have many friends. But his younger brother, Theo, was one of them. As he grew up, Vincent became interested in drawing—and he was very good at it.

In 1886, Vincent Van Gogh moved to Paris to live with his brother, Theo, who collected and sold paintings. In Paris, he met other artists and was influenced by their work. He also became interested in Japanese art and collected woodblock prints.

In 1888, he moved to Arles, a town in southern France. The artist Paul Gauguin moved there too, and they became good friends. But they didn't have much money. Van Gogh often became sad and could not paint.

After a while, Van Gogh recovered and began to paint again. He sent some paintings to Paris, but he could not sell them. Then, in 1890, early on a Sunday evening, Van Gogh went out to the countryside with his paints. He took out a gun and shot himself in the chest. In his short, sad life, Van Gogh painted 200 paintings. He sold only one of them.

B Guidance for Writing (page 72) On a separate sheet of paper, write these headings to divide into topics the autobiography you plan to write. Under each heading, write notes of facts that belong in that section. Then refer to those notes as you write your autobiography.

Some headings:
My parents   My birth   My childhood
My studies   (other)

To describe an event, be sure to provide descriptive details that express the four senses:

sight The fireworks are like beautiful red and yellow flowers in the sky.
There is a huge parade with thousands of people, and everyone is smiling.

sound As you walk down the street, you can hear music and people singing.
The fireworks are as loud as thunder, and you have to cover your ears.

smell You can smell the meat grilling on the street.
Everything smells delicious, and you can't wait to eat!

taste The pastries are as sweet as honey, and you can't stop eating them.
The dish has the sour taste of lemon.

> **Try using these patterns in some of your details.**
>
> **like**
> This traditional dessert looks **like** a beautiful white cloud.
> **as ... as**
> When it is in season, this local fruit is **as sweet as** sugar.
> **so ... that**
> The decorations in the street are **so colorful that** you feel like a child seeing them for the first time.

A On a separate sheet of paper, write a sentence that expresses one of the four senses for each of the following topics. Try to use <u>like</u>, <u>as . . . as</u>, and <u>so . . . that</u> in some of your sentences.

1 Describe a smell in someone's kitchen.

2 Describe a sound in your classroom.

3 Describe the taste of your favorite food.

4 Describe the taste of something you liked as a child.

5 Describe something you see early in the morning.

6 Describe something you hear at a park.

7 Describe something you see at a park.

B Guidance for Writing (page 84) On a separate sheet of paper, write the names of the two holidays you chose for Exercise E. Then, under the name of each holiday make a list of sights, sounds, smells, and tastes associated with it. Use these details in your writing.

UNIT 8 *Summary statements*

When a piece of writing contains several paragraphs, the ideas are often summarized in a paragraph at the end. Including a final **summary statement** reminds the reader of the main ideas that were presented. Read the short essay to the right. Notice the summary statement at the end.

After a problem or a breakdown, many drivers say, "If I had only had a spare tire, I would have been able to fix it and be on my way in a few minutes."

Here are the things responsible drivers should never forget: A flashlight with working batteries can help you repair your car in the dark. A spare tire can save you hours of waiting for help. And remember: you can't change that tire without a jack. If your car breaks down at night, flares can warn oncoming traffic that you are stopped. And if your battery dies, jumper cables can help you start the car again.

No matter how high-tech a car you have, breakdowns can happen at a moment's notice. However, we can plan ahead and be equipped with some simple technology to prevent a problem from becoming worse.

A Read the following piece and underline the main ideas. Then write your own summary statement.

There are a number of excellent presentation graphics technologies available today. Two well-known ones are Microsoft Office's PowerPoint™ and Macintosh's Keynote™. No matter which technology you use, here are some do's and don'ts that will make your presentation more successful.

First, the do's: Keep your slides concise. Keep the amount of text to a minimum because it's hard for the audience to focus on your main points if there's too much text. Use large letters (from 18 to 48 points) and simple, easy-to-read fonts. Use bullets to separate items in a list. Use just a few colors and keep that color scheme consistent throughout the presentation. If your presentation will be in a bright room, light-colored text on dark backgrounds will be easiest to read.

What should a presenter avoid? Don't use all capital letters. They are hard to read. Never use dark letters on a dark background. The presentation will be hard to see. Don't use sound effects that are unrelated to the meaning of your presentation and avoid distracting transitions.

When presenting from a PowerPoint or Keynote presentation, look at your computer screen or handheld notes, not the screen the audience is looking at—to do that you would have to turn away from your audience and you would lose contact with the people you are presenting to.

Your summary statement:

_____

_____

_____

B Guidance for Writing (page 96) After you have completed writing about the advantages and disadvantages of your invention, circle the main ideas in each paragraph. Use the main ideas to write a summary statement for your final paragraph.

The following language helps organize information by contrasting it. It signals to the reader that a contrasting idea will follow.

in contrast
on the one hand / on the other hand
however
nevertheless
even though

A technique to help organize contrasting ideas is to make two lists: **pros** (arguments in favor) and **cons** (arguments against).

To the right are handwritten notes a student made to prepare an essay that presents arguments for and against the mandatory use of a motorcycle helmet. The actual essay can be organized in two ways:

1) as paragraphs in which each of the pros and cons are presented together in contrasting sentences, or
2) as two paragraphs with the ideas in favor in one paragraph and ideas against in another.

Pros
—injuries will be less serious in case of accidents
—lives will be saved
—medical costs will be lower in case of accidents
—people don't have good judgment, so the government has to make decisions for them
—looks cool

Cons
—it limits a person's freedom
—people should drive carefully to prevent most accidents
—if people think they are protected and safe from injury when they use a helmet, they might not drive carefully
—the government shouldn't interfere in the decisions of adults
—messes your hair

A The following essay is organized into two paragraphs. Read the essay and write the main idea of each paragraph.

Should motorcycle drivers be required to wear helmets?

Main idea:

　　Many cities and countries have laws requiring motorcycle drivers to wear a helmet. In some ways these laws are good and effective. For example, it is well known that motorcycle driving is very dangerous. If a motorcycle collides with another vehicle, the driver of the motorcycle has no protection and is often injured or killed. Most fatal injuries are caused by the driver's head hitting the pavement. **On the one hand**, such injuries are often not survivable. **But on the other hand**, if a driver is wearing a helmet, the chance of fatal head injury is reduced. Unfortunately, **even though** drivers know that helmet use could save their lives, many think an accident won't happen to them. **However**, if there is a law requiring drivers to wear helmets, a lack of judgment won't matter. Drivers will have no choice but to wear the helmet.

Main idea:

　　Nevertheless, there are arguments against compulsory helmet-use laws. Some people feel that wearing a helmet causes drivers to have a false sense of security. In other words, drivers may feel that when they are wearing a helmet, they don't have to drive carefully. With a helmet, they feel they have a justification for reckless driving. **In contrast**, other people object to helmet laws because they feel that the government shouldn't interfere with the decisions of adults. They argue that if they get hurt, it's their own responsibility and if they die, it doesn't hurt anyone but themselves. People who have this opinion often complain about government intrusion in personal freedom.

B Guidance for Writing (page 108) On a separate sheet of paper, write the issue you chose and make a list of pros and cons. Use your notes to organize and write your essay.

To describe a place, organize details according to spatial relations. Choose a starting point (for example, the capital city or the largest city). Describe its location.

Lima is the capital of Peru. It is located on the west coast, **on** the Pacific Ocean.

The largest city in China is Shanghai. It is located in the southeast, **along** the South China Sea.

Describe where things are located in relation to that point. Choose a logical order to follow, such as north to south or west to east, so it is easy for the reader to understand.

- **To the [north] of**
  To the north of São Paulo is the city of Campinas.
- **In the [south] of**
  In the south of the island is the city of Kaosiung.
- **[East] of**
  East of Tokyo is the city of Chiba.
- **Next to**
  Next to Washington, D.C. is the city of Baltimore.
- **In the middle / center of**
  In the center of the country is the city of Madrid.

- **Along the [coast / river]**
  Along the coast, and west of the capital, are the cities of Valparaíso and Viña del Mar.
- **At the start of**
  At the start of the Pan-American Highway is the city of Fairbanks, Alaska.
- **At the end of**
  At the end of the Volga River is the Caspian Sea.

A On a separate sheet of paper, write a description for each of these places, using the language above. Use the maps of Guatemala (page 112), Australia (page 113), and Alaska (page 121).

1 Cobán (page 112)
2 Denali National Park (page 121)

3 Sydney (page 113)
4 Mexico (page 112)

5 Alice Springs (page 113)
6 Juneau (page 121)

B Guidance for Writing (page 120) On a separate sheet of paper, draw a simple map of the place you chose in Exercise D. Write numbers on your map for at least two important places, beginning with 1 for the location you will start from, 2 for the next location, and so on. Then, use your map to help you write your descriptions, using the language of spatial relations.

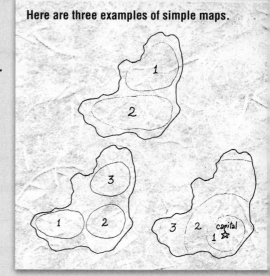

Here are three examples of simple maps.

Top Notch Pop Lyrics

1:16/1:17

🔊 It's a Great Day for Love [Unit 1]

Wherever you go,
there are things you should know,
so be aware
of the customs and views—
all the do's and taboos—
of people there.
You were just a stranger in a sea of new faces.
Now we're making small talk on a
first-name basis.

(CHORUS)
It's a great day for love, isn't it?
Aren't you the one I was hoping to find?
It's a great day for love, isn't it?
By the time you said hello,
I had already made up my mind.

Wherever you stay
be sure to obey
the golden rules,
and before you relax,
brush up on the facts
you learned in school.
Try to be polite and always be sure to get
some friendly advice on proper etiquette.

(CHORUS)

And when you smiled at me
and I fell in love,
the sun had just appeared
in the sky above.
You know how much I care, don't you?
And you'll always be there, won't you?

(CHORUS)

1:33/1:34

🔊 X-ray of My Heart [Unit 2]

Thanks for fitting me in.
This heart is killing me.
Oh, that must hurt.
Are you in a lot of pain?
Yes, I thought I'd better
see someone right away.
It might be an emergency—
could you try to explain?

(CHORUS)
Give me something to keep me
from falling apart.
Doctor, won't you please
take an x-ray of my heart.

You know, I'm here on business,
and today I saw a guy …
Why don't you have a seat
while I do some simple tests?
Thanks. As I was saying,
he walked by without a word.
So that's what's bothering you—
just go home and get some rest!

(CHORUS)

The minute that I saw him
I felt weak in the knees.
Are you dizzy, short of breath?
Does it hurt when you sneeze?
Yes, I have all those symptoms—

and a pain in my chest.
Well, love at first sight
can have painful side effects.
Now, I might not be able
to go to work today.
Could I get a prescription
for some kind of medicine?
Well, let's have a look now.
You might have to heal yourself,
or try another treatment
for the kind of pain you're in.

(CHORUS)

2:17/2:18

🔊 I'll Get Back to You [Unit 3]

Your camera isn't working right.
It needs a few repairs.
You make me ship it overnight.
Nothing else compares.
You had to lengthen your new skirt,
and now you want to get
someone to wash your fancy shirts
and dry them when they're wet.
Come a little closer—
let me whisper in your ear.
Is my message getting across
to you loud and clear?

(CHORUS)
You're always making plans.
I'll tell you what I'll do:
let me think it over and
I'll get back to you.

You want to get your suit dry-cleaned.
You want to get someone
to shorten your new pair of jeans
and call you when they're done.
I guess I'll have them print a sign
and hang it on your shelf,
with four small words in one big line:
"Just do it yourself."
Let me tell you what this song
is really all about.
I'm getting tired of waiting while you
figure it out.
I've heard all your demands,
but I have a life, too.
Let me think it over and
I'll get back to you.
I'm really reliable,
incredibly fast,
extremely helpful
from first to last.
Let me see what I can do.
Day after day,
everybody knows
I always do what I say.

(CHORUS)

2:31/2:32

🔊 A True Life Story [Unit 4]

The story of our lives
is a real page-turner,
and we both know
what it's all about.

It's a fast read,
but I'm a slow learner,
and I want to see
how it all turns out.

(CHORUS)
It's a true life story.
I can't put it down.
If you want to know who's in it,
just look around.

The story of our lives
is a real cliffhanger.
It's hard to follow,
but boy, does it pack a thrill—
a rollercoaster ride
of love and anger,
and if you don't write it,
baby, then I will.

(CHORUS)

You can't judge a book by its cover.
I wonder what you're going to discover.
When you read between the lines,
you never know what you might find.
It's not a poem or a romance novel.
It's not a memoir or a self-help book.
If that's what you like, baby, please
don't bother.
If you want the truth, take another look.

(CHORUS)

3:17/3:18

🔊 Lucky to Be Alive [Unit 5]

(CHORUS)
Thank you for helping me to survive.
I'm really lucky to be alive.

When I was caught in a freezing snowstorm,
you taught me how to stay warm.
When I was running from a landslide
with no place to hide,
you protected me from injury.
Even the world's biggest tsunami
has got nothing on me,
because you can go faster.
You keep me safe from disaster.
You're like some kind of hero—
you're the best friend that I know.

(CHORUS)

When the big flood came with the
pouring rain,
they were saying that a natural
disaster loomed.
You just opened your umbrella.
You were the only fellow who kept calm
and prepared.
You found us shelter.
I never felt like anybody cared
the way that you did when you said,
"I will always be there—
you can bet your life on it."
And when the cyclone turned the day
into night,
you held a flashlight and showed me the safe
way home.

You called for help on your cell phone.
You said you'd never leave me.
You said, "Believe me,
in times of trouble you will never be alone."
They said it wasn't such a bad situation.
It was beyond imagination.
I'm just glad to be alive—
and that is no exaggeration.

(CHORUS)

3:31/3:32
🔊 I Should Have Married Her [Unit 6]

She was born with talents
in both literature and art.
It must have been her love of books
that first captured my heart.
We both had experience
with unhappiness before.
I thought we would be together
for rich or for poor.

(CHORUS)
I should have married her.
She was the love of my life,
but now she's someone else's wife.
I thought we would be happy.
I thought our love was so strong.
I must have got it all wrong.

It's hard to make a living
when you're living in the past.
I wish we could have worked it out,
but some things just don't last.
I wonder what she's doing
or if she thinks of me.
One day she just changed her mind.
The rest is history.

(CHORUS)

It's too late for regrets.
She's gone forever now.
We make our plans,
but people change,
and life goes on somehow.

(CHORUS)

4:18/4:19
🔊 Endless Holiday [Unit 7]

Day after day,
all my thoughts drift away
before they've begun.
I sit in my room
in the darkness and gloom
just waiting for someone
to take me to a tourist town,
with parties in the street and people dancing
to a joyful sound.

(CHORUS)
It's a song that people sing.
It's the laughter that you bring
on an endless holiday.
It's the happiness inside.
It's a roller coaster ride
on an endless holiday.

I try and I try
to work hard, but I
get lost in a daze,
and I think about
how sad life is without
a few good holidays.

I close my eyes, pull down the shade,
and in my imagination I am dancing in a
big parade,
and the music is loud.
I get lost in the crowd
on an endless holiday.
It's a picnic at noon.
It's a trip to the moon
on an endless holiday,
with flags and confetti,
wild costumes and a great big
marching band,
as we wish each other well
in a language we all understand.
The sky above fills with the light
of fireworks exploding, as we dance along
the street tonight.

(CHORUS)

4:34/4:35
🔊 Reinvent the Wheel [Unit 8]

You've got your digi-camera with
the Powershot,
Four mega pixels and a memory slot.
You've got your e-mail and your Internet.
You send me pictures of your digi-pet.
I got the digi-dog and the digi-cat,
the "digi" this and the "digi" that.
I hate to be the one to break the news,
but you're giving me the "digi" blues,

(CHORUS)
And you don't know
the way I really feel.
Why'd you have to go and
reinvent the wheel?

You've got your cordless phone and
your microwave,
and your Reflex Plus for the perfect shave.
It's super special, top of the line,
with the latest new, cutting edge design.
You've got your SLR and your LCD,
your PS2 and your USB.
I've seen the future and it's pretty grim:
they've used up all the acronyms.

(CHORUS)

I keep waiting for a breakthrough innovation:
something to help our poor communication.
Hey, where'd you get all of that high-tech taste?
Your faith in progress is such a waste.
Your life may be state of the art,
but you don't understand the human heart.

(CHORUS)

5:21/5:22
🔊 We Can Agree to Disagree [Unit 9]

I believe that dogs should be
allowed to wander free.
That may be true, but don't you think
that people have rights, too?
I believe that time has come
for true dog liberty.
I see what you mean, but I don't
share your point of view.

(CHORUS)
We can agree to disagree
about what's wrong and right.

It wouldn't be cool for you and me
to fight when we don't see eye to eye.

I think my cat deserves to eat
a treat, no matter what.
Well, on the one hand, yes,
but on the other hand, well, no.
Don't you feel that every meal
should be shared with a pet?
That's one way to look at it,
but I don't think so.

(CHORUS)

You can be a radical.
You can be conservative.
My dog doesn't care, and he won't ask you
to leave.
You can be a moderate.
You can be a liberal.
You can believe what you want to believe.
I urge you to think it over
before you decide.
That your dog is very nice,
I couldn't agree more.
I believe that you and I
should be the best of friends.
That's exactly what I think.
Why weren't we friends before?

(CHORUS)

5:45/5:46
🔊 It's a Beautiful World [Unit 10]

The path is located
half an hour west of here.
I heard it's a must-see,
and that it goes pretty near
to a breathtaking beach
a little farther up the coast.
That's the one that everybody
seems to like the most.

(CHORUS)
It's a beautiful world.
Be careful as you go.
The road is dark and dangerous.
Be sure to take it slow.
Yes, it's a beautiful world,
from the mountains to the seas.
Through life's lonesome valleys,
won't you come with me?

Are you planning on going
to see the waterfall?
I've been thinking about it,
and I want to do it all!
Would you happen to know
anything about Rocky Cave?
How do you get there?
Can you show me the way?

(CHORUS)
I can't wait.
I don't want to miss it.
There isn't a place worth seeing
that I don't want to visit.

(CHORUS)